DISTRUST

AMERICAN STYLE

Sheila Kennedy (signature)

DISTRUST

AMERICAN STYLE

Diversity and the
Crisis of Public Confidence

SHEILA SUESS KENNEDY

Prometheus Books

59 John Glenn Drive
Amherst, New York 14228-2119

Published 2009 by Prometheus Books

Inquiries should be addressed to
Prometheus Books
59 John Glenn Drive
Amherst, New York 14228–2119
VOICE: 716–691–0133, ext. 210
FAX: 716–691–0137
WWW.PROMETHEUSBOOKS.COM

13 12 11 10 09   5 4 3 2 1

Library of Congress Cataloging-in-Publication Data

Kennedy, Sheila Suess.
    Distrust, American style : diversity and the crisis of public confidence / Sheila
Suess Kennedy.
        p.   cm.
    Includes bibliographical references and index.
    ISBN: 978-1-59102-708-9 (pbk. : alk. paper)
    1. Trust—United States. 2. Pluralism—United States. 3. Interpersonal
relations—United States. 4. Politics, Practical—United States. I. Title.

BJ1500.T78K46 2009
320.97301'9—dc22

                                                                    2008054559

Printed in the United States of America on acid-free paper

CONTENTS

INTRODUCTION

W e live in an era with remarkable access to data of all kinds. Scientists uncover the secrets of the physical universe on an almost daily basis; social scientists slice and dice statistics and study populations with a mathematical precision our ancestors could never have imagined. We are literally drowning in facts and figures. Whether this abundance of information has made us any wiser is, of course, a different question.

At its most basic level, this book is about what we know and how we interpret what we know—about how we make sense of the bewildering amounts of information that research and technology are making increasingly available to us. But it is also about what implications we can draw from that information about our country and our uniquely American approach to living together.

7

One of the more obvious problems with data-driven research in a world that is changing and morphing as rapidly and dramatically as ours is the inevitable time lag: by the time studies of populations and their characteristics are available, they provide at best a snapshot of a point in time already past. That time lag is particularly problematic when the pace of social change is accelerating. An even more daunting problem with data interpretation is theoretical. When we look at our empirical findings and study the evidence we have painstakingly accumulated, how do we decide what it means? How do we use it to make public policy?

When you think about it, policy making is a lot like the practice of medicine. Our ability to solve social problems, like our ability to cure disease, depends upon whether we've made an accurate diagnosis of what is wrong. But just as the same set of symptoms can suggest the presence of radically different underlying conditions to different medical specialists, the same "facts on the ground" will be taken by scholars in different academic disciplines and political figures with different ideological perspectives as evidence of very different social problems, and will call forth very different policy prescriptions. Evidence of social dysfunctions involving America's growing diversity is one such case, and the contending scholarship and politics around that issue is the specific focus of this book.

Because scholarship—like reality—is messy, I want to provide a "road map" to what you will find in the pages that follow. I also want to make my own hypotheses—and biases—clear. Political scientists have accumulated a significant amount of data suggesting that over the past decades, Americans have become less trusting of each other, and that as our population's diversity increases, our trust in our neighbors declines. Social scientists warn us that this erosion of interpersonal social trust has very negative implications for our ability to govern ourselves effectively.

I do not dispute the raw data, but I interpret it quite differently. In the following pages, for reasons I will elaborate, I argue that—partly because of the complexities of modern society, and partly because of specific attributes of American political culture—"generalized social trust" is dependent upon our ability to *trust our social and governing institutions.* If my hypothesis is correct, the cure for what ails us does not lie in current efforts to reverse our growing diversity. The remedy does not lie in increasing limits to immigration, nor in building a wall between the United States and Mexico, passing "English Only" laws, or enacting legislative declarations to the effect that America is a "Christian Nation." The remedy is to make our governmental, religious, and civic institutions trustworthy again. And—as I will also argue—we cannot do that without recognizing the role of government as an essential "umpire," enforcing the rules of fair play and setting the standard for our other institutions, both private and nonprofit.

In the course of this discussion, I will draw on many different areas of scholarship in an effort to test my thesis against a variety of different perspectives. I make no pretense that my exploration of these different "ways of knowing" is anything but illustrative (and thus, from the standpoint of academic rigor, superficial.) Think of what follows as a survey course, or a tasting menu, rather than an in-depth exploration of any particular scholarship or discipline. This book is an effort to get a purchase on an aspect of our contemporary civic life that is and has been the subject of much political concern and controversy—to stand back and make a good-faith effort to define our terms more carefully, to consider contending explanations for the evidence at hand, and to see a broader picture.

In short, the book that follows is political, not academic, although I will draw on quite a bit of academic scholarship and research. I say it is political because my argument 1) posits the importance of trustworthy political and legal structures to our ability to live peacefully and productively in an increasingly pluralistic society, and 2) incorporates a political perspective—not in the sense of partisan politics, but in the larger sense of being grounded in a particular set of political questions, and informed by a liberal democratic worldview. As religious sociologist Art Farnsley put it, in an e-mail exchange on the subject:

> Sociologists recognized some time ago that a modern, industrial form of interdependence was replacing the overlapping, more homogeneous social forms associated with small towns. (Tonnies' *Gemeinschaft* and *Gesellschaft*.) There's still overlap, but the emphasis is on interdependence rather than shared, common values and worldviews.
>
> Our world has been shaped by modern, impersonal interdependence for some time. But politics still works much too much on vestiges of shared values. (For example, our deep disputes over issues like gay marriage.) That's a problem in and of itself. To a lot of people, it feels like the "old way" of commonality is slipping out from under them when in fact, it's mostly already gone and they're not preparing to live in an interdependent rather than an overlapping world.[1]

My own academic training was in law, and for practicing lawyers, the question is always, inevitably, "What should we do?" If Art's analysis is correct—and there is much evidence to suggest that it is—what are the implications for our public policies? What should we do as a nation, and a world, to accommodate our human differences and live interdependently and productively? What can various scholarly disciplines teach us about our situation, and what course of action does my particular reading of the data suggest?

WHAT COMES NEXT?

Is it increasing diversity that threatens the social and cultural solidarity Americans require, or is it the failures of our governing institutions? That is the central question I explore in the pages that follow. Any effort to answer that question leads to many others: What are the attributes and cultural norms that Americans really need to share? Why? Do different kinds of diversity, or different amounts, have different effects upon our common civic culture? What is culture? What is "social capital" and why do we need it? Although I make no pretense of providing answers to all of these questions, I do hope that some of the analysis in the pages that follow will provide an entry point, at least, into further exploration of these and related issues.

In chapter 1, I lay out the parameters of the growing and acrimonious debate about the effects of America's growing diversity, focusing first upon recent scholarship suggesting that ethnic diversity increases social distrust (findings that inadvertently give credibility to closet racists, not to mention scolds like Lou Dobbs, Pat Buchanan, and the other voices loudly urging policy makers to build fences around the country to keep "them" out). I then turn to a discussion of the substantial research that would seem to raise a set of different questions about social trust, or that would contradict the conclusions being drawn. It is important that we ask the right questions about social trust in the context of our growing diversity, because—as I argue in chapter 1 and throughout the book—this is a genie that has escaped the bottle. Diversity is a fact of modernity; it is not going away. We aren't going to live in an America that is hermetically sealed off from the rest of the world, and we aren't going to maintain even the degree of racial and economic segregation that continues to characterize many of our neighborhoods even today. If there is one thing researchers all agree on—whatever their discipline or political perspective—it is that America is going to experience more diversity of all sorts, not less. Furthermore, our understanding of what diversity is will continue to change: previously marginalized groups will emerge to press for equality and recognition; religious groups will continue to divide and subdivide; people of different races and ethnic backgrounds will continue to marry and their children will not fit neatly into the demographic categories to which we are accustomed. The task at hand is to manage our differences within a more generous, more capacious understanding of who "we" are. Chapter 1 is an effort to describe what the scholarship tells us about the effects of our differences, the role and importance of social trust, and the process of social change.

In chapter 2, I take a broad look at the ways in which human culture and the process of socialization interact to shape people's individual worldviews, or "mental paradigms," and I investigate the psychological and sociological reasons we may feel threatened or uncomfortable—or distrustful—when we are with people who don't share our particular worldviews. I also consider how paradigms "shift" during times of social change, and the nature of the discomfort that accompanies such shifts. Chapter 2 is an overview, a "macro" look at the ways in which cultures condition human cognition and interaction.

If chapter 2 is "macro," chapter 3 is "micro." In this chapter, I look at the specifics of our American culture and describe some of the ways in which our particular constitutional structure and underlying political philosophy have shaped our distinctive national values. Chapter 3 is an exploration of what I have elsewhere called "the American Idea." In very fundamental ways, that American Idea grows out of assumptions that are antithetical to the theory that Americans need to learn how to trust each other. In chapter 3, and throughout this book, my central argument incorporates a lesson drawn from American history, a history that strongly suggests that the United States is built on a foundation of *distrust*, a foundation of checks and balances, of—at most—conditional trust. To put it another way, we do need trust in order to function, but the nature of the trust we need is (justifiable) confidence in the integrity of our common social and legal *institutions*, not trust in the predictability and responsiveness of our neighbors. In chapter 3, I discuss the philosophical foundations of our government, its genesis in the Enlightenment, the founders' insistence upon structural mechanisms intended to ensure accountable and trustworthy governing institutions, and describe how those constitutive choices have shaped a specifically American culture, and a specifically American approach to the question "How can different people best live together?"

Chapters 4 and 5 consider the importance of government in a diverse and often distrustful society. What is government's role in building trust and social capital? How well have our governing institutions discharged those obligations? Have American elected officials pursued policies or behaviors that are actually destructive of social trust, and if so, which policies are those and how should they be changed? In chapter 4, I analyze an unlikely culprit, the "privatization" and "reinventing government" fad that has grown over the past thirty years. Chapter 4 looks specifically at the consequences of privatization in what has been called "the Indianapolis experiment," and discusses more general research into the unintended consequences of "hollowing out" not just government, but a substantial segment of the nonprofit and voluntary sector. If healthy and functioning government agencies and a robust civil society are necessary to the maintenance of trustworthy institutions, such "hollowing out" makes their task infinitely more difficult.

While chapter 4 suggests how well-meaning but poorly understood policies can undermine social capital, chapter 5 is a critical examination of the effects of government corruption and incompetence. The chapter begins with a whirlwind tour of America's social dislocations since the tumultuous 1960s, the decade that most scholars pinpoint as the time social trust began to decline, and describes the role played by successive presidential administrations in the various political scandals and upheavals that engulfed the nation. Government— beginning with its response to Vietnam War protests and the Watergate scandal during the Nixon administration and culminating in the disaster that has been the George W. Bush presidency—bears a great deal of responsibility for the national mood. Chapter 5 concludes with an (incomplete) litany (some might say diatribe) of the legal, social, and constitutional depredations of the Bush administration, which have been widely reported and have created a national backlash of rather astonishing (and in my view, gratifying) proportions.

In chapter 6, I explore the character and dimensions of what some scholars have referred to as the "trust gap." That is, although it is true that national trust levels have declined since we first began measuring such things, it is equally true that levels of social trust have never been uniformly distributed. In this chapter, I explore who trusts more and who less, and draw on the available literature to offer some theories that may explain those differences.

Finally, in the concluding chapter, I offer some modest proposals for ameliorating our current, arguably untenable, situation. I consider what we might do to restore trust in our essential political institutions and thus return a modicum of trustworthiness to our governing institutions and stability to our body politic.

THE ALL-IMPORTANT CONTEXT: AWASH IN INFORMATION

It is always tempting to assert that we live in times that are radically unlike past eras—that somehow, the challenges we face are not only fundamentally different than the problems that confronted our forebears, but also worse; to worry that children growing up today are subject to more pernicious influences than children of prior generations. (In Stephanie Coontz's felicitous phrase, there is a great deal of nostalgia for "the way we never were.")[2] I grew up in the 1950s and can personally attest to the fact that all of our contemporary, misty-eyed evocations of that time are revisionist nonsense. The widespread belief that '50s-era Americans all lived like the characters who populated television shows like *Father Knows Best* or *Leave It to Beaver* is highly inaccurate, to put it mildly. (Ask the African Americans who were still relegated to separate restrooms and drinking fountains in much of the American South, or the women who couldn't get equal pay for equal work or a credit rating separate from their husbands.)

Nevertheless—even conceding our human tendency to overstate the effects of social change for good or ill—it is impossible to understand any of the issues with which this book is concerned without recognizing the profound social changes that have been wrought by communication technologies, most prominently, albeit certainly not exclusively, the Internet. We live today in an incessant babble of information. Some of that information is transmitted through hundreds of cable and broadcast television stations, increasing numbers of which are devoted to news and commentary twenty-four hours a day, seven days a week. In our cars, we tune in to news and commentary on AM or FM stations, or more recently to satellite broadcasts that have extended the reach of that broadcast medium. But it is the World Wide Web that has had the greatest impact on the way Americans live their daily lives. We read news and commentary from all over the world online, we shop for goods and services, we communicate with our friends and families, and we consult Web-based sources for everything from medical advice to housekeeping hints to comedy routines. When we don't know something, we Google it. The Web is rapidly becoming a repository of all human knowledge—not to mention human rumors, hatreds, gossip, trivia, and paranoid fantasies. Picking our way through this landscape requires new skills, new ways of accessing, sorting, and evaluating the credibility and value of what we see and hear. It is not an exaggeration to say that the enhanced communications environment has changed the way we process information and our very perceptions of reality.

A very minor example may illustrate the point. Toward the end of her life, my mother was in a nursing home. Given the limited mobility of most of the residents, the television was a central focus of their day, and it was on continuously. Although she had never been a particularly fearful person, nor one who focused on crime, my mother became convinced that crime rates were soaring. They weren't. In fact, data confirmed that there had been a substantial decline in the incidence and severity of criminal activity in the United States over the preceding few years. But when mother was growing up, with the exception of particularly heinous incidents from around the country, or crimes involving celebrities or other public figures, the media to which she had access reported on only local criminal behavior. Seventy years later, the television at the nursing home relayed daily reports of subway murders in London, train bombings in Spain, and assorted misbehaviors of people from all over the globe. To my mother and her elderly peers, it seemed that predators were suddenly everywhere.

The Internet has had an infinitely greater impact than has television, which merely extended the way in which we passively receive information. When I am driving to a location I've not previously visited, I get directions via the Web (assuming I don't have a GPS in my car or—more recently— in my cell phone). I can "chat" via Instant Messaging with my granddaughter in Wales, and for free—no long-distance telephone charges incurred. I'm kept up-to-date on what my friends and family members are doing via Facebook. Increasingly, I shop online for books, office supplies, even clothing and home furnishings. We no longer visit the department of motor vehicles and wait in line to renew our license plates— we go online and save the time and trouble. My husband spends hours on Google Earth, marveling at development patterns in Beijing or Dubai. If we want to know how a member of Congress or city council member voted, the information is at our fingertips. In short, the Internet has not only made the world a smaller place, it has also forever altered the rhythm of Americans' daily lives.

The ubiquity of information available to us is only a small part of the transformation we are experiencing. Another huge difference is that we are no longer passive consumers of information; the interactive nature of the Web allows us to talk back, to post our opinions, to offer rebuttals. It brings us into contact with people of different countries, religions, cultures, and backgrounds. (The very name "World Wide Web" is evocative of both its range and connective nature.) The Internet also allows each of us, if we are so inclined, to become a publisher of our own work or that of others. When I was young, the costs of establishing a new media outlet were astronomical; if you wanted to publish a newspaper, the costs of the printing press and distribution system were prohibitive, and most broadcast radio and television stations were owned by the wealthy. Only elites could afford to participate in the business of information. Today, anyone with access to the Internet can hire a few reporters or "content providers" and create her own media outlet. One result is that the previously hierarchical nature of public knowledge is rapidly diminishing. The time-honored "gatekeeper" function of the press—when journalists decided what constituted news and what was thus worthy of reporting—will soon be a thing of the past, if it isn't already.

The communication revolution is not limited to the delivery of news or the provision of other information. Chat rooms, and more recently social networking sites, have allowed like-minded people to connect with each other and form communities that span traditional geographical and political boundaries. (The growing global hegemony of the English language has further enabled cross-national communications.) As a result, it has become much harder to define just what a "community" is.

The participatory nature of the Internet has also encouraged—and enabled—a wide array of political and civic activism. Early in the development of the Web, naysayers worried that the Internet was encouraging people to become more solitary. They warned that people were being seduced by this new medium to withdraw from human and social interaction. In some cases, that was undoubtedly true. (Of course, books have seduced people ever since Gutenberg invented the printing press.) For many others, however, the Internet has been an "enabler," facilitating a great wave of political and community organizing; it has become a mechanism for finding like-minded people we didn't previously know, even though they might have been living just down the street. "Meetings" online have led to Internet-facilitated "Meet Ups" and other face-to-face interactions in service of particular social and political goals.

In the political realm, especially, the transformation has been dramatic. As the Pew Project on the Internet and American Life has documented, in 2008 "a record-breaking 46% of Americans have used the internet, email or cell phone text messaging to get news about the campaign, share their views, and mobilize others." Pew researchers found that 35 percent of Americans had watched online political videos (triple the number who had done so in 2004). Eleven percent had forwarded or posted someone else's commentary on the race. The impact of YouTube and other video sharing sites has been particularly consequential.

A telling example of the change YouTube has wrought in the political landscape was the widely reported "macaca" moment of Senator George Allen during the 2006 campaign season. Allen, who was running for reelection to the Senate from Virginia, was considered a shoo-in, and a strong contender for the 2008 Republican presidential nomination. While delivering a speech to a small gathering in rural Virginia, he pointed out a volunteer from his opponent's campaign, who was videotaping his talk.[3]

> "This fellow here, over here with the yellow shirt, macaca, or whatever his name is. He's with my opponent. He's following us around everywhere. And it's just great," Allen said, as his supporters began to laugh. After saying that [his opponent James Webb] was raising money in California with a "bunch of Hollywood movie moguls," Allen said, "Let's give a welcome to macaca, here. Welcome to America and the real world of Virginia."[4]

Depending on how it is spelled, the word *macaca* can mean either a monkey that inhabits the Eastern Hemisphere or a town in South Africa. In some European cultures, *macaca* is also considered a racial slur against African immigrants. The Webb volunteer (an American whose parents had emigrated from India) promptly uploaded the videotape of Allen's remarks to YouTube; a mere three days later, it had been downloaded and viewed 334,254 times. It was picked up and endlessly replayed on the evening news. Print media across the country reported on the controversy, and radio talk show hosts argued about the meaning of the word *macaca*, and whether Allen had intended a slur. (Allen's own clumsy attempts to "explain away" the reference didn't help.) Investigative reporters whose curiosity had been piqued by the controversy dug up evidence of prior racially charged incidents involving Allen. By November, James Webb—initially dismissed as a long-shot candidate with little chance of defeating a popular sitting senator—was the new senator from Virginia, and "macaca moment" had entered the political lexicon as shorthand for a gaffe captured on video.

As I write this, the 2008 presidential campaign is in full swing, and "viral videos" have been front and center. Singer-songwriter will.i.am of the group Black-Eyed Peas created a music video, "Yes We Can," based upon a phrase from Barack Obama's speeches. For a time, it was everywhere—forwarded and reforwarded until literally millions of Americans had seen it. Humorous and not-so-humorous videos promoting and panning the candidates are ubiquitous. Campaign rumors (and worse) are endlessly forwarded, circulated, and recirculated. John McCain, who has admitted to never using a computer, and who has thus far displayed some discomfort with the new media environment, has on several occasions been caught off-guard by an Internet campaign documenting "flip-flops" in his positions with videos showing him delivering inconsistent statements. (It is troubling to think that a person who is admittedly unfamiliar with the single most consequential innovation of our time may be elected to lead this country. I would argue that failure to understand the impact of the Internet is failure to understand the world we live in. This was undoubtedly the point of a pro-Obama blogger's characterization of McCain as "an analog candidate for a digital age.") All of the political candidates are making extensive use of e-mail to raise funds, organize volunteers, counter charges, announce endorsements, and rally their respective bases, at a tiny fraction of the cost of direct mail. The impact of all this would be difficult to exaggerate.

In 2004, a post on *Politico*, a popular political blog, read as follows:

> Democracy in America is changing. A new force, rooted in new tools and practices built on and around the Internet, is rising along the old system of capital-intensive broadcast politics. Today, for almost no money, anyone can be a reporter, a community organizer, an ad-maker, a publisher, a money-raiser or a leader. If what they have to say is compelling, it will spread.

In a post dated just four years later, in June of 2008, the authors of the original post looked back at those words, and marveled that, if anything, they had vastly *underestimated* the degree of political and social change the new medium would usher in:

> We've lost count of all the national figures that have been affected by online activism. Millions of small donors, people giving less than $200 per donation, have flooded into the presidential campaign process. Far more people are making, watching and sharing online content—from blogs to video— than are visiting the candidates' online websites. And well more than half the electorate, especially the young, is relying on the internet rather than traditional news sources such as newspapers or TV, for political information.[5]

The results of this sea change were evident in the Howard Dean campaign in 2004, but they have been especially apparent in the 2008 presidential campaign. It is hard to imagine that Barack Obama could have defeated Hillary

Clinton, the establishment candidate for the Democratic nomination, without his highly sophisticated use of the Internet to organize volunteers and raise previously unheard-of sums of money. As I write this, the Obama campaign claims nearly a million and a half discrete donors, the vast majority of whom have given less than one hundred dollars. The Internet has thus seemingly accomplished what successive legislative efforts to reform campaign finance failed to do: it has eliminated candidate's reliance on large donors and the disproportionate influence that accompanied that reliance.

It would be a mistake, however, to think that fundraising is the only political change effected by the Internet. The ability to communicate cheaply and almost instantaneously with millions of people, the ability to link up campaign volunteers, and the ability to both spread and counter misinformation have all had a profound impact on our political process, and will continue to change our political, civic, and personal relationships in ways we cannot yet fully anticipate or appreciate. Our common civic landscape is also undergoing profound transformation, becoming more accessible, more "lateral," and more democratic. We won't know the precise contours of that transformation for many years, but it provides the context within which everything in this book must be understood. Its impact cannot be overstated.

This information revolution is particularly pertinent to the issue of trust in our civic and governing institutions. At no time in human history have citizens been as aware of every failure of competence, every allegation of corruption or malfeasance. Politicians like to talk about "low-information" voters, but even the most detached American citizen cannot escape hearing about institutional failures on a daily basis, whether it is reports of high levels of lead in children's toys (said to be due to government failure to monitor imports properly), the collapse of a bridge in Minnesota (said to be due to government failure to inspect and repair deteriorating infrastructure), or vivid pictures of American military men and women abusing prisoners at Abu Ghraib prison (evidence of either incompetent management or outright lawlessness on the part of the Bush administration). It may be true that past eras have experienced similar problems, but it is certainly the case that knowledge of public wrongdoing or incompetence is infinitely more widespread in today's wired and connected world.

The pervasiveness of information—and disinformation—in our brave new world is the subtext of all that follows.

NOTES

1. Art Farnsley, e-mail communication to author, June 2, 2008.

2. Stephanie Coontz, *The Way We Never Were: American Families and the Nostalgia Trap* (New York: Basic Books, 1992).

3. The practice of having campaign workers videotape an opponent's public remarks is another indication of the changes wrought by our electronic communications technologies. Campaigns routinely upload their own speeches and any remarks by their opponents that conflict with prior positions or are otherwise thought to be damaging. This would have been unimaginable even a decade ago.

4. Michael D. Shear and Tim Craig, "Allen on Damage Control After Remarks to Webb Aide," *Washington Post*, August 16, 2006, A1.

5. Andrew Rasiej and Micah Sifry, "See? The Web is Changing Politics," *Politico*, June 12, 2008, http://www.politico.com/news/stories/0608/11014.html (accessed August 30, 2008).

Chapter 1

"TRUST ME," SAID THE SPIDER

"**C**an't we all just get along?" Those wistful words—spoken by Rodney King, whose savage beating by Los Angeles police in 1991 was videotaped by a passerby and repeatedly televised—have entered our national vocabulary. They seem to capture the current American mood. Why are so many of us so hostile? Why do we seem to have so much trouble communicating? Why are we so cynical about business practices, so suspicious of government at every level? Why don't we trust each other?

The question of trust has become a hot topic, not just for the talking heads who increasingly dominate our airwaves, but in academia as well. Questions abound: What do we mean by trust? How does trusting your husband differ from "generalized social trust"? Why is the latter important? How necessary is it to effective governance? Do contemporary Americans really trust their neighbors less than their parents and grand-parents did, and if so, why?

Any serious exploration of these issues requires that we understand the outsized influence of Robert Putnam. Putnam is a highly respected political scientist, whose work has shaped opinion not only in academic circles but also among the so-called chattering classes, the pundits who increasingly frame public perceptions. His best-selling book, *Bowling Alone*,[1] was enormously influential—not only did it introduce the concept of "social capital"[2] to readers who had previously never heard the term, but it also influenced an entire cohort of scholars, foundation executives, and public officials to target and address issues of civic engagement. The book inspired spirited responses, pro and con, and spawned a mini-industry of hand-wringing and doomsday predictions.

Putnam's central concern in *Bowling Alone* was a perceived reduction in the rate at which Americans are participating in communal and political life. He tracked and reported a steadily declining involvement in the voluntary, civic organizations— bowling leagues, PTAs, garden clubs, and the like—through which Americans have traditionally formed social networks. His research documented declines in the frequency of such activities as in-home bridge and poker gatherings, as well as participation in social and political organizations, and showed significant increases in the numbers of Americans who not only bowled alone, but ate alone as well, and did so at imper-sonal, fast-food restaurants rather than at convivial neighbor-hood watering holes. Putnam warned that our increasingly solitary pursuits posed a danger to those "networks of trust and reciprocity" that characterize a healthy polis. Television was singled out as a major culprit and pivotal innovation, giving it an importance reminiscent (at least to some of us of a certain age) of Marshall McLuhan's *Global Village*[3] and Newton Minow's "Vast Wasteland" speech.[4]

Bowling Alone certainly had its critics, both in the popular press and in the academy. A number of scholars faulted Putnam's methodology and challenged his conclusions. In an acerbic article in the *American Prospect*, Garry Wills suggested that the reality of social change is considerably more complicated than Putnam had acknowledged, and that he "should look harder at major social and economic reconfigurations affecting urbanization, education, professionalization, information technology, the family and the work force." We eat out more, Wills pointed out, because more women work outside the home all day—a social shift that arguably creates workplace connections having their own value as incubators of social capital.[5]

Much of the criticism of Putnam's theorized decline in social capital echoed Wills in suggesting that participation in civic organizations overall had not really declined, but had instead changed in character. Those bygone bowlers may be found coaching youth soccer; many of the women who have abandoned the Ladies' Garden Club have defected to professional associations and the local chamber of commerce. Even before the advent of Facebook, MySpace, and similar social networking Internet sites, Robert Wuthnow suggested that Americans are changing the definition of engagement, that we are experimenting with "looser, more sporadic, ad hoc connections, in place of the long-term memberships in hierarchical organizations of the past."[6] That phenomenon has accelerated with the ubiquity of electronic communications; in the jargon of the times, it has "gone viral."

Whatever one's conclusions about the existence and/or severity of the crisis in civic engagement posited by Putnam, *Bowling Alone* clearly struck a nerve. Perhaps because ours is—and has always been—a remarkably heterogeneous country, Americans have long been consumed by the question "What is it that holds us together?" Tocqueville's admiration for our early tendency to form "civic associations" suggested one approach to answering that question.[7] If we create common ground with our fellow-citizens by engaging in recreational, civic, and political activities with them, data that seems to suggest a marked decline in such activities should be taken seriously. Right or wrong, by introducing an important issue to the broader public for consideration and debate, Putnam performed an important public service.

More recently, Putnam's research has led him to an even more disconcerting conclusion: people who live in more ethnically diverse communities are less trusting of their neighbors than are people living in more homogeneous precincts. And they are less trusting of everyone, not just of those who belong to other ethnic groups. If his original findings were controversial, his current research has set off a firestorm. Opponents of immigration (legal or not), multiculturalism (even in its mildest forms), and interfaith dialogue have seized upon the research as vindication of their worst fears. You can almost hear Pat Buchanan urging Americans to dig that moat.

What is the fuss all about? In "E Pluribus Unum: Diversity and Community in the Twenty-first Century," Putnam reports on a recent large-scale study he conducted in which he found a negative correlation between levels of ethnic diversity and generalized social trust. As he puts it, "In the short to medium run, immigration and ethnic diversity challenge social solidarity and inhibit social capital."[8] (In a memorable phrase, Putnam says that in the short term, diversity brings out the "turtle" in us— causes individuals to "hunker down" in their shells and withdraw from many kinds of social interaction.) In the United States, the article has been seized upon by opponents of immigration as evidence that a continued influx of "others" will corrode the social fabric and doom the civic enterprise.

Clearly worried about triggering such a reaction, Putnam takes pains in the article to emphasize the limited nature of the research and the potential for positive outcomes. He cautions that his study—like all surveys—reflects responses given at one specific point in time, and thus does not and cannot predict what he terms "long-term" attitudes. As he points out, America's entire history is a story of how, in the face of successive waves of immigration and substantial social conflict, we have managed to emerge with a broader, more inclusive sense of who "we" are. As communities become more diverse, trust may decline, but other research shows enhanced levels of creativity and economic growth. And most basic of all, he reminds readers that *correlation* is not the same thing as *causation*. Just because diversity and distrust coincide is not evidence that one has caused the other.

All of that is true; however, I have a hunch that Putnam's empirical findings—so far as they go, an important qualifier—are essentially correct. For reasons we will explore, I think it unlikely that the existence of ethnic diversity alone can explain the decline in social trust. (Available scholarship raises more questions than it answers about diversity. In "Trust, Inequality and Ethnic Heterogeneity," Andrew Leigh found distrust to be more pronounced when there was linguistic heterogeneity than when differences were limited to ethnicity. He also found that in Australia, unlike America, there was no relationship between economic inequality and distrust.[9] Others have found a high correlation between education and social capital[10] generally correlates with higher income.) But I also have a theory about why diversity probably contributes to that decline—a theory that I will discuss in much more detail in chapter 2.

Cognitive sociologists tell us that people are most uncomfortable when they are forced to question the "taken for granted" nature of their worldviews. If that is true (and a lot of research suggests that it is), discomfort with increased diversity—at least, certain *kinds* of diversity—makes perfect sense, as we will see. When we assume that most people think the way we do—because they look like us, or go to our church, or bowl in our league—we trust others more, even those we don't know, because we take it for granted that they see the world in pretty much the same way we do. Sometimes that's true; often it's not.

When we live in communities where we are forced to confront obvious differences, as with race, ethnicity, or culture, we are also forced to confront the fact that other people bring different worldviews to the social table. We suddenly realize that different people occupy different realities. Eventually, it dawns on us that *everyone* is a unique, and at some level unknowable, individual—that it isn't just those who look or sound different. We begin to realize that we always have to start at square one, that we always have to evaluate people—even those of "our own kind"—on their individual merits. We can't just make assumptions about their attitudes or likely behaviors based on skin color or religion or sexual orientation and expect that those will be accurate. The "taken for granted" element is gone, and relations with others lose a degree of spontaneity as we consider probabilities, risks, and options. As a result, many of us will retreat a bit—or "turtle"—around people we don't know, whatever their appearance or ethnicity. This is rarely a conscious process; the only thing we are conscious of is that we no longer simply take for granted that we know what others will think and how they are likely to react, and we are accordingly a bit more guarded. The "taken for granted" element of our interactions is what allows us to feel comfortably at home in our environments, and to act reflexively and without undue hesitation—an important component of trust. (Of course, what we are trusting is as much our own ability to predict the behavior of others as it is a belief in the trustworthiness of those others.)

The two questions I will consider in the pages that follow

are 1) whether this decline in generalized social trust, assuming it has occurred, is primarily an outcome of America's increased diversity, or whether other aspects of our contemporary civic experience may be equally—or more—responsible; and 2) whether the nature of the social trust America requires at this particular juncture in our national evolution is different from that needed in simpler, more rural communities, and if so, why and how. Addressing those questions requires considering several others: What kind of trust does our society require? Why? When might trust itself be dangerous to our civic health? Under what circumstances? When is trust important, and when is it problematic? And perhaps most important, how do we build a trustworthy society?

In the chapters that follow, I will argue that we need to conduct this discourse about trust with appropriate recognition of the magnitude and pace of social change and the multiplying complexities of contemporary American life. I will argue that a certain amount and kind of *dis*trust is not only healthy, it's actually the American Way. And finally, I will argue that when our governing institutions betray the central insights of the Founding Fathers—insights that are critical to our ability to create *unum* out of our *pluribus*—our political communities and trust levels suffer accordingly.

DEFINING OUR TERMS

Putnam believes that social trust—the belief that other people in your neighborhood and community are generally trustworthy—is essential to social capital. In order to understand what all the hand-wringing is about, it's important to understand not only what social capital is, but also what role it is thought to play in society. Simply put, *social capital* is the name we give to our memberships in social networks, the variety of human relationships within which we are embedded. The term is thought to have been coined by Jane Jacobs in her seminal study of urban life, *The Death and Life of Great American Cities.* In order to describe the characteristics of good city neighborhoods, Jacobs drew on a fiscal analogy:

> To be sure, a good city neighborhood can absorb newcomers into itself, both newcomers by choice and immigrants settling by expediency, and it can protect a reasonable amount of transient population too. But these increments or displacements have to be gradual. If self-government in the place is to work, underlying any float of population must be a continuity of people who have forged neighborhood networks. These networks are a city's irreplaceable social capital. Whenever the capital is lost, from whatever cause, the income from it disappears, never to return until and unless new capital is slowly and chancily accumulated.[11]

As one scholar of the concept puts it, "To have social capital, a person must be related to others, and it is those others, not himself, who are the actual sources of his or her advantage."[12] Anyone who has ever found a job—or a car, or a spouse—through networking with friends and colleagues has benefited from social capital.

Trust is an important component of social capital, but reciprocity is also an essential element. To explain the concept of reciprocity, Putnam has quoted the philosopher David Hume:

> Your corn is ripe today; mine will be so tomorrow. 'Tis profitable for us both, that I should labour with you today, and that you should aid me tomorrow. I have no kindness for you, and know you have as little for me. I will not, therefore, take any pains upon your account; and should I labour with you upon my own account, in expectation of a return, I know I should be disappointed and that I should in vain

depend upon your gratitude. Here then I leave you to labour alone; You treat me in the same manner. The seasons change; and both of us lose our harvests for want of mutual confidence and security.[13]

We require trust and reciprocity among participants in our social networks because collaboration and collective action are at the heart of the concept of social capital. As Carles Boix and Daniel Posner have written, "Social capital is, at its core, a set of institutionalized expectations that other social actors will reciprocate cooperative overtures."[14] If we fail to work together when such collective efforts are necessary, we all emerge the poorer. Without trust that our participation will be reciprocated, we are less willing to enter into communal enterprises. Even government, with its monopoly on the legitimate use of coercive power, cannot implement programs effectively in the absence of social capital and voluntary compliance; there is a limit to how much can be accomplished only by the use of authority and control, as many an autocrat has unhappily discovered.

Closely allied to the concept of social capital is that of civil society—what Nancy Rosenblum has called the "chicken soup of political theory."[15] Civil society, sometimes called the nonprofit and voluntary sector, is composed of human networks that are neither governmental nor individual. (Most students of the concept would argue that social capital networks are not exclusively those created by the organizations in civil society— that we can build social capital through workplace associations, for example. But civil society is where the great majority of such networks are found). The sometimes dizzying array of voluntary and nonprofit associations that make up civil society are thought to act as a buffer zone between the large and frequently impersonal institutions of formal government, on the one hand, and the individual and his or her family, on the other. These institutions also facilitate civic and collective activities that are nongovernmental in nature. Francis Fukuyama has described the "left-wing" version of civil society as a community-wide mobilization to stop a new Wal-Mart. A "right-wing" version might be an antitax protest that defeats funding for construction of a new high school.[16]

As Arthur Brooks has pointed out, although there is a good deal of empirical evidence demonstrating a connection between the health of the nonprofit sector and the effectiveness of our government institutions, there are two contradictory theories about the nature of that relationship. Putnam and those who agree with him argue that reduced participation in civil society leads to disengagement from politics and governance.[17] Other research, however, asserts that higher confidence in government predicts higher levels of participation in the various institutions of civil society.[18] It is the classic conundrum of the chicken and the egg, and the conclusions we draw will depend upon which of these two theories we find most persuasive.

In all of the discussions of the benefits of communal activities and civil society—and they are many—we shouldn't lose sight of the fact that social capital can be a two-edged sword. In particular, we must recognize the differences between the two kinds of social capital, between what has been called *bonding* social capital and what is known as *bridging* social capital. Bonding social capital encourages in-group solidarity. When we think of the bonds forged in kinship groups, church "families," fraternal organizations, and the like, we see the positive side of bonding social capital; its negative aspects are apparent in groups like the Black Panthers and the Ku Klux Klan. Bonding capital tends to reinforce exclusive identities and homogeneity, to solidify the conviction that there is a "we" that is distinct and apart from "them," while bridging social capital promotes ties across group barriers. Bridging social capital refers to the sorts of relationships forged in service clubs, political organizations, and other venues where we come together with a more diverse group of our fellow citizens in order to accomplish a particular task, or support a particular institution or cause. To borrow the language of political philosophy, we might say that bonding social capital is characterized by "thick" connections, and bridging capital by "thin" ones.

The "thick" networks that distinguish bonding social capital can be very useful; these are the kinds of networks that tend to reinforce discipline and provide moral and material support to individual members. The unit cohesion of a military battalion, the pride and shared sense of accomplishment exhibited by members of a sports team, and exhibitions of patriotism at times of national crisis are generally considered to be positive manifestations of bonding capital. On the other hand, bonding networks can lead members to exclude outsiders, promote conformity, and restrict individual liberty. When the members of that battalion feel obliged to cover up criminal conduct by their compatriots, when the members of the sports team show disdain for those who aren't as athletic, or when patriotic displays degenerate into nationalist braggadocio and unilateralism, we see the negative aspects of bonding social capital.

Bridging social capital empowers individuals by extending the networks to which they have access and by encouraging social cooperation across lines of ethnicity, religion, and other categories of personal identity. But bridging capital is weaker: the social ties thus formed involve lower levels of trust and reciprocity, and correspondingly less social support, than is true with the thicker bonding forms of social capital. We are unlikely to feel as much solidarity with the friends we make at the meetings of Save the Whales as we feel with members of our families, or with our ethnic group, or the soldiers with whom we have shared battle.

With both bonding and bridging social capital, trust and

reciprocity are considered key, but there is a lively debate about which is more important to the kind of social capital that contributes to overall social health. One of the more acute participants in that debate is Marc Hooghe, a Belgian scholar who has argued that too much attention has been paid to the element of trust, and not enough to reciprocity, which is "better adapted than trust to function in divided, plural and increasingly diverse societies." Hooghe points out that reciprocal relationships can encourage cooperative ventures, which in turn can generate an ongoing relationship founded upon a "process-based" form of trust. He also notes that reciprocity enjoys something of a competitive advantage over trust, since it can operate in conditions of uncertainty and diversity.[19]

Hooghe is also one of the many scholars who point out that there are many different kinds of trust, and they are not equally pertinent to the creation of social capital. Are we talking about interpersonal trust, which depends on knowing the character and previous behavior of a friend or colleague? Or are we talking about the sort of "generalized" trust that—as several students of the concept have pointed out—depends heavily on resemblance and homogeneity? That kind of trust "has to be achieved within a familiar world."[20]

> The central role of reputation and stereotyping also implies that closed networks will be much more conducive in developing trust than open and rapidly fluctuating networks.[21] The closure of networks has a double impact on the decision to trust. First, it allows for a more effective sanctioning of behavior. . . . Secondly, reputation (and gossip) travels faster in closed networks than in open environments.[22]

The argument here is that what Hooghe calls "depersonalized trust" (i.e., trust of someone with whom we don't have any history or prior relationship) is possible *only* with bonding

eminently rational response to the realities of contemporary urban life, where neither word of mouth nor signals of similarity are available, trustworthy shortcuts for making individualized judgments.

Rather than composing odes to a bygone day, rather than bemoaning the loss of interpersonal trust of the sort experienced in smaller communities where (like Sam's bar in *Cheers*) "everybody knows your name," contemporary communities have compensated for urban complexity and attempted to accommodate the realities of modern city life by creating trustworthy institutions. Not that this process has been intentional or deliberate—far from it. Rather, it has been an evolutionary change. As societies have grown larger and more complex, the repositories of social trust have shifted. That shift has been adaptive, as biologists might put it. But as valuable as trustworthy social institutions are, and as critical to the operation of modern life, they are different *in kind* from the trust repositories of simpler times, and they require different strategies to ensure that they remain trustworthy. Gossip and reputation will not alert investors to unsound practices in the banking sector, nor to the machinations of an Enron, Tyco, or WorldCom.[27]

THE PARADOX OF INSTITUTIONAL TRUST

Where does government fit in all of this, if it does? Government is the largest and most important—not to mention the most pervasive—of our collective social mechanisms. As we will see in chapter 3, this nation's founders crafted governing institutions that were constrained by structural guarantors of good behavior. The monarchies with which they had experience had provided plenty of examples of unconstrained—and untrustworthy—behavior, and it was their explicit goal to provide safeguards against similar abuses by the new government they were creating. The Founding Fathers saw government's role in classically libertarian terms: it was a necessary collective mechanism to deal with external threats, and to prevent some citizens from harming the persons or property of others. But they were well aware that a government powerful enough to provide security would be a government powerful enough to threaten that same security. They did not place their trust in the goodness of the people who would be elected to run that government—they placed it in the checks and balances they created. For good measure, they added the Bill of Rights.

Gradually, as America grew larger and more complicated, the government has assumed additional responsibilities. Many of these new duties came as a result of the Great Depression, and the recognition that citizens needed an "umpire," a trustworthy institution to police and regulate a variety of business practices. Even the most ardent contemporary advocate of limited government is likely to concede the utility and propriety of FDA regulations of food quality, for example, in an era when few of us grow our own vegetables or slaughter our own animals. (I'm pretty libertarian, but I personally do not want so much "freedom" that I have to test the chicken I buy at the local supermarket for *E. coli*. I prefer to trust the FDA.) Americans today rely on government agencies to ensure that our water is drinkable, our aircraft flyable, our roads passable, and much more.

It would be difficult to overstate the importance of our being able to trust our government agencies to discharge these and similar functions properly. When Americans go through a time where government seems inept or corrupt, as we periodically do, that confidence is shaken, and our skepticism and distrust affect more than just the political system. That is because trust in government institutions sets the tone for our confidence in *all* institutions. When we perceive that our government is not trustworthy, that perception infects the entire society. There was a reason the United States experienced so much upheaval and social discord in the wake of the Watergate scandal.

And of course, it isn't only government. Thanks to the vastly expanded reach of communications technologies, twenty-four-hour "news holes," blogs, and the like, it is the rare American who is not bombarded daily with news of corporate malfeasance, the sexual escapades of "pro-family" legislators and errant pastors, the identity of the latest sports figure to fail a drug test, and more. Those technologies also provide platforms and megaphones for some of the least civil denizens of the "chattering classes," pontificators who routinely inform us of the thoroughly rotten—and untrustworthy—behaviors of our governing institutions, our neighbors, our churches, and competing elements of the mass media.

From time to time, America has gone through periods where the failures of our civic and governing institutions and those who are managing them have been so manifest that knowledge of them is simply inescapable. We are in one such period as I write this, with one important difference: the amount of information possessed by even the most "low-information" members of the public has been enormously amplified by the explosion of communications technologies. The American public is positively marinating in bad news, and the national "malaise," as Jimmy Carter might have phrased it, is palpable. That sour national mood affects each of us. As Putnam has repeatedly acknowledged, causation is rarely uni-dimensional. We cannot overlook the effects of these constant revelations of corruption and/or incompetence on the overall levels of generalized trust.

Think about it. We live in a time when many of our most important institutions have been publicly compromised. Media figures who were supposed to be independent watchdogs are found to be writing administration propaganda, and getting paid handsomely for it, and it turns out that pundits who have been making impassioned arguments for Policy X have been raking in handsome "honoraria" from companies that stand to benefit from Policy X. Headlines report lawsuits against the Catholic Church for protecting priests accused of being sexual predators. Religious authorities decry the "politicization" of Evangelical congregations and the co-option of conservative churches for partisan political ends; at the same time, there has been a series of widely publicized "outings" of Evangelical clergy—stories that several of the movement's most prominent (and most insistently antigay) preachers have themselves been embroiled in homosexual liaisons. When we turn to the business news, each day seems to bring a new round of scandals—whether it is retirees losing their pensions, oil companies making obscene amounts of money while continuing to profit from special tax breaks, reports of predatory lending practices, or the recent crisis caused by subprime mortgage foreclosures, it is a rare day when some widespread, unsavory conduct is not uncovered.

Meanwhile, the Bush administration's open disdain for constitutional checks and balances and the rule of law has given rise to unprecedented—and justifiable—alarm. Even if one discounts the multiplying charges of illegal and unethical behaviors, the conduct of the war in Iraq and the massive failure of federal, state, and local government agencies to deal competently with the destruction caused by Hurricane Katrina have shaken confidence in government reliability at all levels.

In the face of so much evidence that we cannot trust our most important institutions to operate honestly and effectively, and in the absence of evidence that we can do much of anything about it, is it any wonder that people are wary, skeptical, and "turtled"?

WHAT DO WE DO?

Fortunately, there is a massive amount of research on the qualities of trustworthy institutions. We can learn from that research, and we can make our government agencies trustworthy again. Trustworthy and responsive governing institutions can in turn address the genuine challenges created by diversity, and can do so more productively. But in order to make use of that knowledge, it is important that we really understand the roots of the problem we face. Repairing our social infrastructure is like fixing anything else; in order to prescribe the proper remedy, we need an accurate understanding of what it is that's wrong.

In the chapters that follow, I will try to provide a context within which to evaluate where we are, where we have been, and where we need to go. Ethnic diversity is a part of that picture, but it is only one part. Its impact on our civic fabric ultimately depends on us, on our ability to understand the nature of the challenges we face, and to separate substance from cant and hyperbole.

NOTES

1. Robert Putnam, *Bowling Alone: The Collapse and Revival of American Community* (New York: Simon & Schuster, 2000).

2. *Social capital* is the term given to human networks that engender mutual trust and reciprocity. Section 2 of this chapter explains the concept in more detail.

3. Marshall McLuhan and B. R. Powers, *The Global Village: Transformations in World Life and Media in the 21st Century* (New York: Oxford University Press, 1989).

4. Newton Minow, "Television and the Public Interest," speech delivered at the National Association of Broadcasters, May 9, 1961 (Pacifica Tape Library).

5. Garry Wills, "Putnam's America," *American Prospect* 11 (2000): 16.

6. Robert Wuthnow, *Loose Connections: Joining Together in America's Fragmented Communities* (Cambridge, MA: Harvard University Press, 1998).

7. Alexis de Tocqueville, *Democracy in America*, ed. J. P. Maier, trans. George Lawrence (Garden City, NY: Anchor Books, 1969).

8. Robert Putnam, "E Pluribus Unum: Diversity and Community in the Twenty-first Century," *Scandinavian Political Studies* 30, no. 2 (2007): 137–74.

9. Andrew Leigh, "Trust, Inequality, and Ethnic Heterogeneity," *Economic Record* 82, no. 258 (2006): 268–80.

10. M. Smith, Lionel J. Beaulieu, and Ann Seraphine, "Social Capital, Place of Residence, and College Attendance," *Rural Sociology* 60 (1995): 363–80.

11. Jane Jacobs, *The Death and Life of Great American Cities* (Atlanta: Vintage Books, 1992).

12. Alejandro Portes, "Social Capital: Its Origins and Applications in Modern Sociology," *Annual Reviews in Sociology* 24, no. 1 (1998): 1–24.

13. Robert Putnam quotes from David Hume's *A Treatise of Human Nature* (Oxford: Clarendon Press, 1888) on p. 134 of his *Bowling Alone.*

14. Carles Boix and Daniel Posner, "Social Capital: Explaining Its Origins and Effects on Government Performance," *British Journal of Political Science* 28, no. 4 (1998): 686–93.

15. Nancy Rosenblum and R. C. Post, *Civil Society and Government* (Princeton, NJ: Princeton University Press, 2002), p. 23.

16. Francis Fukuyama and IMF Institute, "Social Capital and Civil Society," *International Monetary Fund, IMF Institute* (2000).

17. Arthur Brooks, "Can Nonprofit Management Help Answer Public Management's Big Questions?" *Public Administration Review* 62, no. 3 (2002): 259–66.

18. Notably a study by J. Brehm and W. Rahn, "Individual-Level Evidence for the Causes and Consequences of Social Capital," *American Journal of Political Science* 41 (1997): 999–1023.

19. Marc Hooghe, "Is Reciprocity Sufficient? Trust and Reciprocity as Forms of Social Capital," presented at the 98th Meeting of the American Political Science Association (September 1, 2002).

20. N. Luhmann, "Familiarity, Confidence, Trust: Problems and Alternatives," in *Trust: Making and Breaking Cooperative Relations*, ed. D. Gambetta, 95 (Oxford: Basic Blackwell, 1988).

21. James Coleman, *Foundations of Social Theory* (Cambridge, MA: Harvard University Press, 1990).

22. Hooghe, "Is Reciprocity Sufficient?" p. 7.

23. Ibid., p. 11.

24. John Tierney, "Facts Prove No Match for Gossip," *New York Times*, October 16, 2007.

25. Paul Krugman, "Will There Be a Dollar Crisis?" *Economic Policy* 22, no. 51 (2007): 435–67.

26. Jane Jacobs, *Systems of Survival: A Dialogue on the Moral Foundations of Commerce and Politics* (New York: Random House, 1992), p. 5.

27. These were just three of the companies that were embroiled in financial scandals during the early 2000s. Their accounting irregularities and self-dealing left thousands of investors with worthless stock, and destroyed the retirement savings and cost the jobs of thousands of employees.

Chapter 2

PLURALISM AND THE PARADIGM PROBLEM

F ear of "the other" has been a constant throughout human history. We have many theories, but few satisfactory answers to the question of why that is. We have even fewer answers to the question "How do we decide who qualifies as 'other' at any given time or place?"

The composition of the American population has changed dramatically since the Puritans made landfall at Plymouth Rock. We are obviously much more densely populated; according to the 2000 census,[1] the United States is home to more than 281 million people, including nearly 35 million African Americans, 2.5 million Native Americans, over 10 million Asian Americans, and 15 million belonging to other, unspecified races. Nearly 7 million people checked the new census form box next to "multiracial." Thirty-five million people, representing a variety of races, were ethnic Hispanics or Latinos. Forty-six million spoke a language other than English at home. Ninety-eight percent of all homes had at least one television set, 51 percent had a computer, and over 40 percent had Internet access (a number that has since skyrocketed). Many more people lived alone than had previously been the case. Average household size had declined to just over two and a half persons, and average family size to just over three. The US population was also aging—the result of both longer life spans and fewer children. Americans were more mobile than ever. And while the census bureau does not collect information on citizens' religious affiliations, the American landscape in 2000 was overflowing with megachurches, cathedrals, mosques, synagogues, and temples. Diana Eck begins *A New Religious America* with descriptions of a mosque outside Toledo, a Hindu temple near Nashville, a Cambodian Buddhist temple near Minneapolis, and a Sikh gurudwara near Fremont, California.

How deeply rooted are the differences between these Americans? How important are those differences in our daily lives? One of the problems with Putnam's conclusion that diversity drives down trust and thus diminishes social capital is that defining diversity can be tricky. The word itself may be one of the most overused terms in our current political lexicon. Depending upon the context, we may describe as "diverse" differences of race, gender, family composition, age, sexual orientation, religion, and country of birth. At times, we also talk about "diversity of opinion" or "diverse perspectives." Technically, *diversity* simply refers to differences within a particular population or population subset; the term may be used to indicate a certain degree of heterogeneity within a group, a "range of variation," or simply "unrelatedness." However, as we all know, some differences are considerably more salient than others, and depending upon the situation and the environment, different kinds of diversity will be considered more or less significant or threatening. Even the effects of racial or ethnic differences—generally considered to be among the more consequential types of diversity—will depend significantly upon other factors, such as education and socioeconomic status.

Some examples may demonstrate the point. I teach at a public university. As a female, I am considered an "affirmative action" hire (that is, I "count" toward the university's goal of gender balance), as are the African American and Asian colleagues with whom I regularly interact. Yet we have an enormous amount in common with each other and with our white male peers. We have, for the most part, been socialized into an academic culture. We all have advanced degrees. We are virtually all middle class and (pay levels in academia being what they are) decidedly middle income. Most of us would describe ourselves as members of the academic "community."

This is not a situation unique to higher education. When I was a practicing lawyer, I had several African American lawyer friends. I had far more in common with them than I did with my (white) plumber or my (white, female) hairdresser, and they had considerably more in common with me than they did with most poor blacks living in inner-city ghettos or (in the case of the criminal defense lawyers) with their clients of any color.

Religious congregations—especially in smaller, more rural communities—include members with different educational levels, different occupations, different recreational interests, and often, different political affiliations. Yet members of such congregations will often describe themselves—and genuinely consider themselves—as members of a close-knit "church community." (On the other hand, the composition of such church "families" rarely spans the racial divide; even in twenty-first-century America, Sunday morning continues to be the most highly segregated time of the week.)

Political activity is another arena in which demographically unlike people come together to work for candidates and policies they all support. American political parties depend upon outreach to a variety of constituencies, on their ability to cast a wide net—or build a "big tent"—in order to win elections. As those of us who've been politically active will attest, many fervent partisans consider other members of their own political party to be part of "us," whatever their ethnicity, race, or religion. They reserve the label "them" for members of the opposing party. And of course, in times of national peril or threat, all other Americans—whether Republican, Democratic, Libertarian, or Green—suddenly are part of "us." In the wake of 9/11, before tragically misplaced national policies drove wedges between Americans, we saw a wave of genuine social solidarity spanning ethnicity, religion, race, and other standard markers of diversity.

What is true of race, gender, and religion is equally true of other aspects of identity. We are all members of different "communities" for different purposes and at different times, and our tendency to define others by reference to any one particular characteristic can be problematic. For example, one of my sons is gay. As he has pointed out on several occasions, one of the pitfalls of being identified primarily through membership in a community that is still defined by its "otherness" (and thus still being denied equal legal rights and social acceptance) is this tendency to define complicated humans having multiple allegiances by a single nonconforming characteristic. Most people are much more than any single aspect of their identity. My son is comfortable with and positive about his sexual orientation, and he is involved with the gay community, but he is, as he says, more than just a gay man, just as he is more than just a blue-eyed man, a Jewish man, or a blogger. At any given time, one or another aspect of our complicated identities will be more or less important to us. Defining people by reference to a single trait, and then pronouncing them different from others by virtue of that definition, is undoubtedly a convenient judgmental shortcut, but it is simply inaccurate.

As I have argued at length elsewhere,[2] the diversity that is most consequential for social capital and political stability is *diversity of worldview*. When people are operating out of different conceptual paradigms, different frameworks of meaning, it becomes difficult to communicate with each other in any meaningful way. It is when we can't communicate, when we don't recognize the frame of reference out of which another person is operating, that we are most aware of the gulf between us, and most conscious of our differences. (This may be one of the reasons that immigrants from non-English-speaking countries seem to trigger such a hostile reaction in some people, while immigrants from places like Canada and Great Britain generally do not.)

Like social capital, effective communication requires a particular kind of trust. We need to have confidence that we are arguing from the same basic premises, that at some level, no matter how minimal, we are able to comprehend what it is the other person is saying and the basis upon which that person is saying it. In other words, effective communication requires that—at least to some extent—we occupy the same reality. The much ballyhooed "culture war" is an example of the sort of conflict that arises when people don't share a reality.

An excellent example of just that sort of conflict occurred in 2003, when in a widely publicized incident, federal courts ruled that a five-ton granite stone bearing a replica of the Ten Commandments must be removed from the entrance to the Alabama Supreme Court. The monument had been placed there by the presiding chief judge, Roy Moore (since removed), who insisted that it was an appropriate recognition of the nation's Christian roots. Supporters rallied for Judge Moore as the Ten Commandments were being removed, and several of them were interviewed by television reporters. Virtually all of them denounced the removal of the monument as an infringement of their "religious freedom." Lawyers and civil libertarians found this claim ludicrous; when they looked at Judge Moore, they saw a theocrat attempting to use the authority of the state to endorse a particular religious perspective at the expense of all others—the absolute antithesis of "religious freedom." It is unlikely that the partisans on either side were intentionally being dishonest. They simply looked at the same set of "facts"—a five-ton stone with a carved replica of the Ten Commandments, located at the entrance to the Alabama Supreme Court, and a federal order to remove it—but they interpreted what they saw in radically different ways. Both genuinely believed the other side was willfully ignoring "plain" truths: Moore's supporters were angry that federal courts would not recognize the "fact" that the United States was a Christian nation. Civil libertarians found Moore's position ridiculous in the face of the First Amendment's "clear" prohibition of religious establishments—a clarity that, needless to say, eluded Moore's defenders.

While it is perfectly possible to have a genuine discussion or even a productive argument about American values—to disagree about which values are sound, or how particular values ought to apply in a particular situation, or which values should trump others—that is not what the argument about Alabama's Ten Commandments monument was about, and it is not what America's "culture war" has been about. Indeed, even the term *values* means very different things to different people; for many, it is a euphemism for arguments over religious doctrine. But the "values debate" or "culture war" is not a conflict between people who are religious and people who are secular, nor is it a struggle between those who hold to different religious beliefs. To the extent that it is real, and not simply being deployed for political gain as a "wedge" issue, it is an argument between people who are operating out of different and inconsistent *worldviews*, people who hold and employ inconsistent conceptual paradigms. Many of the culture warriors who are arguing with each other most strenuously—and unproduc-tively—look alike. They would not fit into the accepted categories of "diversity" used by social scientists, yet their differences are far more salient than my differences with my Asian colleagues, or my son's differences with his straight friends.

WHAT ARE WORLDVIEWS AND WHERE DO THEY COME FROM?

How often, when you are watching talking heads on television, or listening to a bombastic radio talk show host, have you wondered, "What planet does that guy come from?" Most of us have had those moments, and they reflect the fact that every human being has a unique mental framework, rooted in his or her most basic beliefs about the nature of reality, and when we don't share a reality, we simply can't comprehend what the other person is saying. Our beliefs, or worldviews, have been shaped in significant part by culture, and human cultures are inevitably rooted in religion. (Throughout human history, religious diversity—whether doctrinal or cultural—has been among our most intractable human differences.) Our worldviews, or mental paradigms, are what academics call "normative concepts," and they shape the way we see the world: our notions of public virtue, our definitions of merit, and our attitudes toward work, family, and community. Many, if not most, of our thorniest public arguments are rooted in these different worldviews into which we have been socialized. Our political positions on everything from the causes of poverty to the appropriate role of the state, the meaning of law, our responsibility for the natural environment, and the role of the United States in international affairs are firmly grounded in the different realities we inhabit.

A personal story may illustrate what I mean. When my middle son was eight or nine, he asked me a question that brought me up short. "Mom," he began, "I say the sky is blue.

You say the sky is blue. But how do we know that we are both seeing the same color? Maybe the color I see is what you call orange, and I call orange blue because I've been taught that blue is what we call the color we see when we look at the sky. How do you know that what you call blue and what I call blue is really the same color?" In that one (unanswerable) question, posed by an inquisitive eight-year-old, is the real problem we face. In order to hear each other, in order to trust each other, we need to know that we share a common reality. We need to know—or at least believe—that we see the same color when we look at the sky. We don't need to share skin color, or gender, or even religious doctrinal belief, but we do need to share, at least partially, a culture and a conceptual paradigm. And that further complicates the issue of diversity, because the "markers" for shared and unshared paradigms, the identities that signal shared cultural understandings or a lack of such understandings, are not necessarily those that social scientists classify as "diversity," although the categories often coincide or overlap.

It is important to be clear about the way I am using the term *religion*. The construction of our culturally shaped worldviews began with the earliest humans' efforts to make sense of natural phenomena. Generally, the explanations they came up with were what we would call religious. For some, thunder and lightning were evidence that the gods were angry; for others, disease and poverty were God's punishments for moral failure. In *The Sacred Canopy*, sociologist of religion Peter Berger wrote: "Every human society is an enterprise of world building. Religion occupies a distinctive place in this enterprise."[3] Berger defined religion as a "humanly constructed universe of meaning," and cautioned that the continuing "plausibility" of any religious world is dependent upon the presence of social structures that are built upon and incorporate that religion's concept of reality. That is, our worldviews can only function in societies where our particular view of reality is taken for granted, seen as self-evident. When social changes or world events threaten our understanding of reality (or, in Berger's phrase, undermine that "plausibility structure"), there is trouble.

I first became aware of how much we take our assumed realities for granted during a conversation with my best friend many years ago, when she was still working on a doctorate in philosophy and was semiobsessed with the nature of knowledge. It was a beautiful day, and we were sitting in an outdoor section of a local restaurant having lunch. I don't recall how the subject came up, but she began explaining that we couldn't possibly know whether the tree next to us was real, or simply an artifact of social convention. I had a moment of disorientation—how would I behave if I were suddenly unsure that the table was solid enough to hold my plate, or if the chair I occupied was a figment of my imagination? I finally responded by saying that it would seem prudent to consider the tree real and to refrain from driving my car into the space it appeared to occupy—just in case.

We all construct our realities; it is impossible not to. It is important to recognize the role culture plays in those constructions, and it is especially important to recognize the immensely important role that religion has played in shaping our various human cultures. Again, I am using the term *religion* here to refer to those systems of ultimate meaning around which substantial numbers of humans have traditionally organized their understandings of reality and of life's purpose. To be religious in this sense is not necessarily to have faith in the supernatural or in a transcendent being, nor does it imply adherence to a specific set of theological propositions. Among the many available definitions of what it means to be religious, some would apply only to systems based upon some conception of deity; for purposes of cultural formation, those definitions are too narrow. Other definitions, however, are so broad as to include virtually any meaningful community ethic or ideology; such a definition is equally unproductive for efforts to understand the nature of human cultures. The definition of religion that I am using grows out of what sociologists call "social function" analysis. In that definition, a religion is a set of beliefs that 1) provides individuals with a meaningful framework for understanding the world, 2) establishes rules governing ethical personal and social behavior, 3) defines the individual's place within society, and 4) legitimizes social policies and institutions.

It is also important to make clear what religious diversity— at least using this definition—*isn't*. The mere fact that you and I attend different churches, synagogues, or mosques, or identify ourselves as members of religions holding different doctrines, does not mean that we necessarily hold different worldviews. In the United States, especially, religious pluralism has operated to moderate purely sectarian disputes like those that led the Puritans to leave England, Roger Williams to found Rhode Island, or Catholics to establish their own schools. Today, interreligious difficulties are most often cultural, and frequently unrecognized. They tend to arise when we simply do not realize that we are operating out of a particular set of assumptions about what "goodness" and "morality" look like, when the basic foundations of my religion (my "meaningful framework") are so fundamentally at odds with yours that I may not even recognize that your particular practices or beliefs are entitled to be classified as religious. As Winifred Sullivan has reminded us, "the traditional American evangelical Protestant definition of religion as chosen, private, individual and believed" now shares space in a pluralist culture in which many other traditions define religion as "given, public, communal and enacted."[4] Pious political references to a "Judeo-Christian" Americanism ignore or trivialize those profound and still-salient distinctions.

A case in point is the language employed in debates over

President Bush's "faith-based" initiative. The term *faith-based* was undoubtedly chosen in an effort to be ecumenical and inclusive; however, it is a term based upon a narrowly Protestant conception of religion—a conception and a terminology that equates religion with faith, and thus excludes (I am sure unintentionally) traditionally "works-based" religions like Judaism and Catholicism, not to mention religions like Buddhism, to which "faith" in this sense is largely irrelevant. Similarly, people who consider themselves entirely secular and nonreligious often share significant worldviews with adherents of some religions, and virtually none with adherents of others. The roots of our contemporary differences are religious only in the sense that they are cultural; they are not traditional doctrinal disputes.

CULTURE AND SOCIALIZATION: DIFFERENT STROKES FOR DIFFERENT FOLKS

Socialization is the process through which we learn "the way things are," the process of learning, unconsciously and unquestioningly, how humans behave. My mother used to tell a joke that illustrates that process perfectly: A young bride is getting ready to cook her first ham for her new husband. In preparation, she cuts the ham in two. Her husband asks why she has cut the ham, and she looks at him blankly—it had never occurred to her that everyone didn't begin to cook ham by cutting it. Finally, she says she really doesn't know why she does it that way, but that her own mother had always cut *her* ham into two pieces before cooking it. She calls her mother and asks, "Mom, why do we cut the ham before cooking it?" Her mother is equally taken aback by the question, and says she really doesn't know, but that *her* mother had always done so. So the bride calls her grandmother and asks the same question. The answer? "I never had a pot big enough to fit a whole ham."

This is how socialization works. We live many aspects of our lives out of force of mental habit, not questioning the reason or purpose, but simply assuming that "that's the way it's done," because that was the way it was done in our homes or communities. For decades, men who worked in offices got up in the morning and tied a piece of cloth around their necks, and never thought to ask, "What's a tie for, and when did men start wearing them?" These automatic behaviors—and there are hundreds of them—serve a purpose; if we actually stopped to consider and question why we do every single thing we do, we wouldn't do very much. Socialization is not only inevitable—it is useful. But sometimes, behaviors that were commonsensical and necessary at their inception, like cutting the ham so that it would fit in the pot, lose their utility over time. Some become counterproductive.

Many of those early ways of doing things are religious in origin. We rarely recognize the extent to which religions have left their imprints on even the most secularized of our modern human cultures and worldviews. In *Sacred and Secular: Religion and Politics Worldwide*, Pippa Norris and Ronald Inglehart wrote that "distinctive worldviews that were originally linked with religious traditions have shaped the cultures of each nation in an enduring fashion; today, these distinctive values are transmitted to citizens even if they never set foot in a church." To illustrate the point, they repeated an amusing but telling exchange with a colleague from Estonia who was trying to explain the differences in worldviews between Estonians and Russians. "We are all atheists; but I am a Lutheran atheist and they are Orthodox atheists."[5]

Sociologists tell us that the function of culture is social control. Our cultures tell us what behaviors are acceptable; they establish collective, authoritative norms that decree which behaviors are appropriate and which are not. In the United States, in addition to our general (and ever-evolving) "American" culture, there are regional subcultures, professional or academic subcultures, ethnic and religious subcultures, and so forth. (To further complicate matters, many of us live within—and move between—several different cultures or subcultures.) A culture "nurtures predictability in social relations" by making and promulgating assumptions about human nature, prescribing expectations for appropriate social conduct, establishing identity, and maintaining boundaries.[6] While religion has been a very important contributor to this process, it is only one of the economic, environmental, and situational factors that interact with each other to shape human cultures. Peter Berger has defined culture as "the totality of man's products," including language and symbols. He reminds us that it is always and inevitably a collective construction dependent upon socialization.[7]

If cultures are the medium through which worldviews are transmitted, worldviews are the mental frameworks (or "conceptual paradigms") that individuals develop as a result of being socialized into a particular culture. We use our worldviews to filter and sort our encounters with external stimuli— if we didn't have those frameworks, those mental categories for filing away information and connecting it to similar data, nothing would make sense—we'd live in a constant, chaotic kaleidoscope of sensory inputs. We might think of our mental frameworks as "habits of the mind" (distinct from, although related to, the "habits of the heart" made famous by Robert Bellah and his colleagues in their book of the same name).[8] They are the cognitive mechanisms through and around which each individual human being defines and coordinates reality. Our individual worldviews are conceptual paradigms produced by the interaction of the "reality structure" of a particular culture with the capacities and experiences of unique individuals.

Paradigm was originally a linguistic term, and it owes its current usage and popularity to Thomas Kuhn, a physicist who, in the course of research for his dissertation, picked up Aristotle's *Physics* and discovered that it made absolutely no sense to him. Since Kuhn assumed that Aristotle wasn't stupid (and since he didn't think that he was stupid, either), he concluded that they were operating out of such different, and inconsistent, realities that communication was not possible. Kuhn was intrigued, and proceeded to write a book about the meaning and use of conceptual frameworks and the way that science adapts or "shifts" its paradigms.[9] Paradigm theory has since been applied to social as well as scientific phenomena, and there are varying claims about how our mental paradigms operate. It has been suggested, for example, that anomalies falling outside our paradigms, or frames of reference, are simply unseen—that is, if we encounter a fact for which we have no place in our conceptual framework, a fact that simply doesn't fit with our understanding of reality, we won't willfully disregard its existence; we simply won't see it because we don't have a mental "place" to put it.

The old story of the blind men and the elephant is an excellent illustration of the way our mental frameworks function. One blind man feels the animal's tail and concludes that an elephant is a type of snake; one of the others encounters the animal's broad side and says no, an elephant is a kind of wall; yet another feels a leg and asserts that both the others are wrong, an elephant is most like a tree. We all use our existing frameworks to make sense of the phenomena we encounter because those frameworks are the only tools we have. If we have no frame of reference for a whole elephant, we will not— we arguably *cannot*—"see" a whole elephant.

Whatever its drawbacks, paradigm theory is a useful way of thinking about diversity, trust, and the multitude of culturally inculcated belief structures that not only help humans make sense of reality, but lead us to categorize some people as "like

"Christian"—or more accurately, Protestant—nation. (In America, as the saying goes, even the Catholics and the Jews are Protestants.) Arthur Schlesinger Jr. once noted that assaults on Western tradition by minorities, academics, and others are "conducted very largely with analytical weapons forged in the West."[18] The bottom line is that we human beings are inevitably and inescapably products of the cultures that create our worldviews; that's what we mean when we say that certain belief systems are hegemonic.

PARADIGM SHIFTS

Cultures and the worldviews they shape do change and evolve and, as I have noted above, that process can be quite painful. Because we take our worldviews for granted, because mental frameworks describe "the way things are," we rarely have reason to doubt or question them. (Obviously it's a tree! What does it *look* like?) When discrepancies arise between our observations or experiences and our mental frameworks, we behave a lot like the blind men with the elephant—we try to "shoehorn" the anomalies into our existing mental paradigms, and we ignore the inconsistencies that result. Sometimes, however, the discrepancies are just too big or too numerous to ignore, and despite our very human resistance to change, our paradigm does shift, transforming the way we see the world. As more and more people shift their paradigms, the dominant worldview prevailing in a culture will change; over time, in some cases, that change is so radical that it will represent "an entirely new view of reality."[19]

> [W]e argue that new social paradigms normally emerge unintentionally, are incompletely and vaguely expressed, and only gradually gain adherents as increasing numbers of

people become aware of the anomalies within the old social paradigm. . . . The tendency for adherents of competing scientific paradigms to "talk past" one another and hence fail to communicate in any meaningful way is even more pronounced with social paradigms.[20]

With the advent of modernity, with increasing diversity and the loss of cultural isolation, the rapidity—and discomfort—of social change has dramatically accelerated. Transportation and communication are in many ways turning the globe into a single community and thereby confronting us all with information that does not fit comfortably within our existing worldviews. We humans resist changing the way we view the world; while different individuals may be more or less receptive to change, most of us are threatened and/or disoriented to some degree by assaults on our habitual understandings of reality and the "taken for granted" nature of our worldviews.

This process of adapting our worldviews and cultures to meet the challenges posed by modernity is sometimes called *secularization*. Many contemporary scholars believe that secularization and individualism were both inevitable outcomes of Protestantism, with its emphasis upon the individual. They believe that a paradigm shift occurred once it was no longer necessary to have an ecclesiastic authority mediate the relationship between the individual and the sacred. The Reformation, and later the Enlightenment, ushered in radically new ways of thinking about science, the nature of reality, and the authority of governing institutions. The Industrial Revolution also brought major social changes. Émile Durkheim argued that industrialization brought plurality and "functional differentiation" in its wake—the separation of areas of authority and expertise that characterize modern societies, and that most of us take for granted. When citizens of modern countries are sick, we call the doctor, not the priest or rabbi; when we want to learn engineering, we study science at the university rather than religious texts at a monastery; when we want to know what the law is, we consult our lawyer, not our spiritual advisor. Religious authority has become steadily less extensive; at the same time it faces increasing competition from other centers of authority and from other systems of belief. Secularization understood in this way has changed the American civic and religious landscape in very important ways, and religious traditions have lost their monopoly on providing ultimate meaning. Secularization in Western society may best be understood as declining religious *authority*, rather than declining religious *belief*. (Although in most parts of Europe, it has come to mean both.) Certainly the sources of moral and religious authority in a highly diverse country like the United States are less monolithic, less culturally dominant.

As our planet shrinks and our pluralism grows, a considerable amount of cultural synthesis is inevitable—especially in a nation where people prize their individuality and their ability to decide for themselves how their lives should be lived. In the United States, capitalism has encouraged a market ethic that now extends from our selection of neighborhoods, foods, occupations, presidents, and mates to our choice of religious and political beliefs. While many of us find that autonomy liberating, and others find it unsettling or even frightening, contemporary Americans enjoy individual choices on a scale unimaginable to prior generations. Our choices are continually expanding, and with that expansion has come increasing differentiation. The current American religious, political, and ideological marketplace is a sometimes bewildering smorgasbord of beliefs and movements from which "consumers" can pick and choose. The degree to which we make choices that alter traditional worldviews (or the degree to which altered worldviews permit us to consider a wider range of choices) depends on many factors. Some individuals feel empowered by the range of options available; others feel threatened. But choice is both a consequence and an engine of change in modern capitalist societies.

One result of living in a society that includes so many competing (and sometimes irreconcilable) worldviews is conflict. There is a constant struggle to "control the narrative"—a struggle for the ability to set the agenda and dictate the nation's dominant worldview. This helps to explain why passions are so engaged in public policy arguments revolving around those agencies of society that are thought to have the most power to set the American agenda: government (especially the Supreme Court), the media, and the schools.

THE QUESTION OF TRUST

What do these complexities of culture, socialization, and pluralism have to do with the theory that as diversity grows, social trust declines? At a minimum, they suggest the need for a more nuanced approach to the nature of diversity. More important, considerations of culture also require us to understand the nature of our own uniquely American culture, and to question the assumption that social trust is an unmitigated good—that anything that diminishes or reduces it is necessarily detrimental to our national interest.

When we analyze the arguments that have been triggered by Putnam's research through the lens of political philosophy, we find that they are not really new. These concerns are part and parcel of a philosophical debate that is as old as Aristotle[21]—a debate that has become steadily more acute since the emergence of the modern nation-state, namely, what are the characteristics of the good society? How much cultural homogeneity is required for humans to flourish and for their societies to function smoothly? What is the proper balance between the individual's right to be different and the degree of cultural uniformity required in order to achieve the common good—and who gets to decide what that degree is, and what "the common good" looks like? Those who crafted America's legal framework struck a balance that favored—and fostered— the very individuality that so bedevils our contemporary culture warriors. The Founding Fathers could not have envisioned the degree of diversity and cultural pluralism that has become a given in today's highly mobile America, any more than they could have imagined cell phones, air travel, or the World Wide Web. The fundamental question raised by Putnam's research is whether the framework they devised, and the balance they struck, is sufficiently durable to withstand the growing pluralism that characterizes our brave new world.

Do our divergent worldviews and the lack of social solidarity and interpersonal trust that those differences imply doom our desire to be part of something larger, part of a coherent collective structure? Or do the reasons for our current social dysfunctions lie elsewhere? Before we can answer those questions, we need to revisit and reconsider America's fundamental assumptions about the nature of legitimate government and the attributes of the good society. And we need to understand how, and to what extent, the choices made then have given shape to the American culture within which we must coexist, and dictated our particular approach to pluralism and human difference.

NOTES

1. 2000 US Census, US Census Bureau.
2. Sheila Kennedy, *God and Country: America in Red and Blue* (Waco, TX: Baylor University Press, 2007). This chapter draws heavily upon the research done for that book.

3. Peter Berger, *The Sacred Canopy* (Garden City, NY: Doubleday, 1967), p. 175.

4. Winifred Sullivan, "The State," in *Themes in Religion and American Culture*, ed. Philip Goff and Paul Harvey, p. 257 (Chapel Hill: University of North Carolina Press, 2004).

5. Pippa Norris and Ronald Inglehart, *Sacred and Secular: Religion and Politics Worldwide* (Cambridge: Cambridge University Press, 2004), p. 17.

6. David Leege and Lyman Kellstedt, *Rediscovering the Religious Factor in American Politics* (Armonk, NY: ME Sharpe, 1993), p. 8.

7. Berger, *Sacred Canopy.*

8. Robert Bellah, *Habits of the Heart: Individualism and Commitment in American Life* (Berkeley: University of California Press, 1985).

9. Thomas Kuhn, *The Structure of Scientific Revolutions* (Chicago: University of Chicago Press, 1962), p. 5.

10. Eviatar Zerubavel, *Social Mindscapes: An Invitation to Cognitive Sociology* (Cambridge, MA: Harvard University Press, 1999).

11. Ibid., p. 67.

12. John Green, "U.S. Religious Landscape Survey," *Pew Forum on Religion and American Life*, February 2008.

13. S. Cotsgrove, *Catastrophe or Cornucopia: The Environment, Politics and the Future* (Chichester: John Wiley, 1982), p. 82.

14. Alan Miller, "The Influence of Religious Affiliation on the Clustering of Social Attitudes," *Review of Religious Research* 37, no. 3 (1996): 230.

15. John Gray, *Men Are from Mars, Women Are from Venus: A Practical Guide for Improving Communication and Getting What You Want in Your Relationships* (New York: HarperCollins, 1992).

16. George Marsden, *Fundamentalism and American Culture: The Shaping of Twentieth Century Evangelicalism, 1870–1925* (New York: Oxford University Press, 1980), p. 213.

17. Robert Bellah, "The Protestant Structure of American Culture: Multiculture or Monoculture," *Hedgehog Review* 4 (2002): 13.

18. Arthur Schlesinger Jr., "The Cult of Ethnicity, Good and Bad," *Time* 26 (1991).

19. M. E. Olsen, D. G. Lodwick, and R. E. Dunlap, *Viewing the World Ecologically* (Boulder, CO: Westview Press, 1992), p. 2.

20. Ibid., p. 10.

21. Aristotle believed that the good society was one that enabled human flourishing. (Of course, different cultures will define "human flourishing" in radically different ways.)

Chapter 3

DISTRUST, AMERICAN STYLE

Before we can consider what America's growing diversity means for our common future, we need to understand this country's unique history and the effect that history has had on our own culture. To begin with, unlike most other countries, the United States is in a very real sense a "manufactured" country. Unlike other nation-states, we are not an outgrowth of kinship groups, and we don't trace our ancestries to a specific piece of territory, a common language, or a common religion. Native Americans excepted, we have always been a nation of immigrants.

DIVERSITY AND DISTRUST IN THE COLONIES

While a majority of the early American settlers were English-speaking Europeans, they were religiously quite diverse, although overwhelmingly Christian: a 1771 woodcut from the collection of the New York Historical Society shows the skyline of New York punctuated with eighteen church spires, to serve a population estimated at less than 22,000. Dutch Reformed, Anglican, and Presbyterian denominations accounted for three each; there were two Lutheran churches, and the French Huguenots, Congregationalists, Methodists, Baptists, Quakers, Moravians, and Jews accounted for one structure each.[1]

Such racial and cultural diversity as existed was provided first by Native Americans, and later by the slave trade. Historian Alan Taylor has detailed the often-neglected pluralism of the American colonial period in *American Colonies*. As one reviewer put it, Taylor's "underlying theme [is] that American distinctiveness lies not in any inherent uniqueness of the British colonial experience of creating new societies, but in the unprecedented mixing of radically different peoples . . . and in the intersection of such a variety of different colonial stories and their eventual convergence into a single national story."[2]

The history of our country has been a continuation of this process of self-invention, a process of incorporating very unlike people into a single national narrative. As I have written elsewhere,[3] America is better understood as an *idea* than a place, and an important aspect of that idea is our willingness to embrace what is new and different—a willingness that is in important respects a legacy of our origins. Thomas Friedman, columnist for the *New York Times*, alluded to the power of that legacy and that idea in a commentary on the extremely positive reactions by Egyptians and citizens of other Middle East countries to the nomination of Barack Obama, a black man with a politically inconvenient middle name ("Hussein") and Muslim ancestry:

> I just had dinner at a Nile-side restaurant with two Egyptian officials and a businessman, and one of them quoted one of

his children as asking: "Could something like this ever happen in Egypt?" And the answer from everyone at the table was, of course, "no." It couldn't happen anywhere in this region. Could a Copt become president of Egypt? Not a chance. Could a Shiite become the leader of Saudi Arabia? Not in a hundred years. A Baha'i president of Iran? In your dreams. Here, the past always buries the future, not the other way around. . . .

Yes, all of this Obama-mania is excessive and will inevitably be punctured should he win the presidency and start making tough calls or big mistakes. For now, though, what it reveals is how much many foreigners, after all the acrimony of the Bush years, still hunger for the "idea of America"—this open, optimistic, and, indeed, revolutionary, place so radically different from their own societies.[4]

What Americans have in common is that idea, that cultural acceptance of a particular approach to difference and innovation, a particular view of how governments should and should not behave, and the responsibilities free citizens should assume.[5] In a very real sense, we are a voluntary community, and voluntariness, while it can be liberating, is a characteristic that leads to a measure of insecurity. As Todd Gitlin has written, "The United States is a nation that invites anxiety about what it means to belong, because the national boundary is ideological, hence disputable and porous." Gitlin refers to this self-identification as "covenanted patriotism, as opposed to the blood and soil variety."[6] As any competent historian will affirm, the forging of a distinctive "American" identity has always been messy and heavily contested. No matter what you learned in kindergarten, the process did not begin with the Puritans and Indians sharing a Thanksgiving turkey dinner and singing *"Kumbaya"*—relations between Native Americans and the early colonists were uneasy even at their best, and they were rarely at their best. Settlers from different countries looked askance at each other. Colonies routinely ejected religious dissenters. The slave trade eventually brought thousands of Africans with different skin colors, religious beliefs, and cultures to America's shores. As the colonies became more populous, they developed distinctive political cultures of their own, and they were competitive with and suspicious of each other. It should thus be no surprise that trust and brotherly love were not the most noticeable features of colonial life.

CONSTITUTIONALIZING DISTRUST

Distrust of English rule led to the Revolutionary War, and distrust among the colonies led the new nation to adopt the largely aspirational Articles of Confederation rather than a constitution that would unequivocally bind those colonies together under a strong national government. It was only when the confederation proved too weak to provide effective governance that the men we collectively call "the Founding Fathers" recognized the need to rectify the weakness and create a "more perfect union." Furthermore, the delegates who gathered in Philadelphia to accomplish that task brought their distrust—of government in general and other colonies in particular—with them. They faced a difficult task: creating a national government that would be strong enough to govern, yet constrained enough to respect the considerable differences among the states—especially the growing differences over slavery, but also substantial religious and political differences.

Checks and balances grew out of the central preoccupation of those charged with creating that new government: limiting the exercise of government power, but without repeating the mistakes of the Articles of Confederation. They were all too aware of the conundrum they faced: a government strong enough to protect citizens' property would be a government strong enough to expropriate that property. Their goal was a central government with enough power to be effective, but not enough to be dangerous, and this was a group of men who were well aware how easily power can corrupt. They were also aware that when government is seen to be playing favorites, when different groups can "buy" privileges and special treatment, civic distrust is the inevitable consequence. Rather than trusting those who would subsequently be elected to manage the new government, they placed their reliance on structural and institutional impediments to mischief. They divided the new government into three coequal branches: a legislative branch to make the laws, an executive branch to administer and enforce them, and a judicial branch to say no when either of the others overstepped its authority. This mechanism, which we refer to as "separation of powers," is best understood as an institutionalized form of distrust, and it is absolutely basic to our constitutional system.

The separation of powers was not the only structural brake the founders placed on the power of the state. Constitutional architects devised several different systems to prevent the new government from becoming autocratic: *federalism,* which further divided power by assigning authority over certain functions to the federal government and continuing to vest others in state and local authorities; *representative* (rather than democratic) government, in which voters elect representatives (or initially, for the Senate, electors who *then* elected the senators) to actually debate and decide policies; and a *bicameral legislature* (a legislature with two houses, with bills required to pass both). All of these mechanisms were intended both to limit the power of the new central government and to temper the "passions" of popular majorities.

When the Constitution was submitted to the colonies for ratification, even the inclusion of all of these impediments to the use and abuse of power were not deemed adequate. The colonists also demanded—and got—a bill of rights. As a result—"power to the people" rhetoric to the contrary— American government does not operate by majority rule. While it is certainly true that a great many of our public decisions are based upon majority preferences, the Bill of Rights is correctly understood as a counter-majoritarian instrument. It was grounded in distrust of majority passions and put in place to protect individuals against the misuse of government power *even when* acting at the behest of those majorities.

The Bill of Rights grew out of the philosophy of the Enlightenment, and it was an institutional recognition of human diversity. Its passage was an effort to protect dissent, individual autonomy, and the right of each individual to be different, to decide for himself or herself what to believe, what to read, and what to think, free of the interference of even a freely elected, majoritarian government. Like the structural checks and balances built into the fabric of the Constitution, it was an outgrowth of the colonists' deep distrust of government, democratically elected or not. The men who drafted the Constitution deliberately chose to include mechanisms that would force deliberation, negotiation, and compromise, that would serve to remind the new government that—as Hobbes had insisted—its primary purpose was to protect individual liberties. In a very real sense, the passage of the Bill of Rights institutionalized (or, as academics might say, "operationalized") an affirmation of human diversity and a deep distrust of official power to enforce conformity.

When we revisit the founding era, we sometimes forget that the founders didn't protect our right to say what we think because they trusted we would all mouth nonoffensive proprieties. They didn't insist on our right to pray (or not) as we choose because they were confident we would all agree about the nature of Ultimate Truth. And they didn't insist that government have a good reason to search or detain us because

characterized the country in earlier times. Libertarians distrust official power much more than contemporary liberals do.

At the other end of the political spectrum, communitarians fault the liberal democratic system for what they believe is an excessive distrust of majority preferences, and an unwise *over*emphasis on the individual and on individual rights. Within the Western liberal tradition, communitarians (like the socialists and communists before them) complain that a neutral state that places process above substance and sees individual moral choice as a private rather than public concern fails to meet the universal and human need for meaning. They contend that liberal theory suffers from an "impoverished vision of citizenship and community."[10] Communitarians take issue with the most fundamental commitment of liberal democracies: that persons should be free to set and pursue their own ends, in accordance with their own values. They argue that freedom, properly understood, is "freedom to do the right thing" and that political community, in order to be experienced and sustained as a true community, must insist upon shared values and an agreement on moral ends.[11] In this view, it is more important that those ends be correct than they be freely chosen.[12]

Communitarians believe that humans are first and foremost social animals, that the relationships within which we are embedded are what give human existence meaning. They deny that public and private activity can be separately categorized, and as a general matter, they would therefore privilege social norms over the individual's right to be different. It is unclear just how much communitarians equate the "society" they want to empower with government; however, most communitarian writers seem willing to trust agencies of the state with far more authority than they enjoy in our particular constitutional system.

In the United States, at least, both libertarians and communitarians would agree that certain fundamental human rights exist and ought to be respected by agencies of the state, but they would strike a very different balance between the power of the majority (however expressed) and the rights of individuals. Communitarians' insistence on shared moral ends have led them to criticize liberal constitutionalism as morally inadequate, because they believe it is all about fair treatment—due process, equal protection—rather than shared goals, about *means* rather than *ends*. Libertarians and liberal democrats, however, respond by arguing that liberalism *does* endorse ends: liberty, individual autonomy, equality before the law, and tolerance. Liberal democracy begins with respect for the value and uniqueness of each individual, and requires behavior consistent with that respect, notably tolerance of those who differ. Liberal political theory values an umbrella understanding of unity, one that can accommodate diversity. It affirms the belief that society is strengthened and enriched by a multiplicity of voices and a constant testing of moral and political theories. In this view, to allow the state to prescribe one particular moral code or to impose political uniformity would violate the conscience and insult the personhood of citizens and—not incidentally—would also foster resentments that would ultimately endanger continued social stability and civic peace.

Whatever its perceived theoretical shortcomings, liberal democracy would seem to be a system tailor-made for the radically diverse populations of the twenty-first century, where agreement on matters of ultimate meaning is unlikely to be achieved. In the American system, we aren't supposed to rely on the good will or forbearance of our neighbors or elected officials when we exercise our human rights; we aren't supposed to trust that they will refrain from treating us badly because we hold minority opinions or identities. Instead, each of us has an enforceable right to those liberties and opinions. So long as our institutions function as originally intended—so long as the safeguards erected to keep the authority of government limited and its operations trustworthy continue to function—we are not required to place our trust in the fallible individuals who may come into positions of authority.

THE CHALLENGE OF MODERNITY

The challenge of diversity—particularly (although certainly not exclusively) the challenge presented by immigrants from countries with very different cultures than our own—is that effective governance must be based upon at least a minimally shared national narrative. Americans need to inhabit a reality that at least partially overlaps with the realities of other Americans; we need to share some (undefined) minimum of common values, or we simply cannot function as a unified society. Many social critics argue that we have already stretched that common fabric too thin, and that the gridlock and hyperpartisanship we see in Washington is the inevitable result.

The communitarians among us blame "radical individualism" for this state of affairs. In contrast to that communitarian critique, in the next few pages I want to defend the proposition that the *only* plausible governing paradigm for America in the twenty-first century is the same constitutionally constrained, liberal democratic system that the founders bequeathed us. Before engaging in that task, however, it is only fair to make as explicit as possible the basic assumptions I bring to the discussion:

- Failure to deal constructively with Americans' deeply rooted racial, religious, and cultural differences is not an option. There are, it seems to me, only three possible consequences of the intense struggle currently being waged for control of America's national narrative: a prolonged and paralyzing inability to forge effective policies or elect leaders whom most citizens can accept as legitimate; reaffirmation of liberal democratic values (including the value of equal respect for those with whom we disagree) as our governing paradigm; or control of the mechanisms of government by those who have power and influence and are willing to use those advantages to ensure the dominance of their particular worldviews.

- While conflict—often impassioned—is inevitable in any society, prolonged, intense intergroup hostility and polarization are undesirable. Equally undesirable, and ultimately unsustainable, is the uniformity or conformity achieved by authoritarian regimes, or through the domination of some by others. That is, while suppression of conflict through the exercise of power may be preferable to open warfare, it is both less desirable and less likely to endure than a peaceful coexistence that respects the equal civil and human rights of others.

- Increased pluralism and contact with people who are racially, ethnically, religiously, culturally, and ideologically different is a fact of modern life. Such contacts will only accelerate; they are inescapable. Communication and transportation technologies and global economic realities make cultural isolation impossible. This inevitable feature of contemporary society will continue to threaten the taken for granted nature of our worldviews.

- Maintaining cultural traditions is important, not just to individuals, but to political communities as well. A nation with no normative culture is untenable—its center cannot hold. But it is also important that subnational communities (religious, ethnic, or cultural) be able to maintain their distinctive identities, insofar as those are meaningful and important to them, and that our national norms include accepting and adapting to the resulting diversity of American cultures and traditions. What we need is a shared national identity that makes room for such communities within a distinctive common culture we call "American."

Liberal democracy has been defined as "a principle of political organization that accords individuals the freedom to navigate a course of their own design, constituted by self-elected plans and purposes."[13] William Galston has argued that liberal societies are characterized by a strategy that minimizes coercion[14] and Ronald Dworkin has defined liberal constitutionalism as "a system that establishes legal rights [to self determination] that the dominant legislature does not have the power to override."[15] Liberal societies are not unrestrained democracies. In *The Future of Freedom*, Fareed Zakaria has reminded us of the significant difference between pure democracy—defined simply as rule by the majority—and liberal democratic regimes, where fundamental liberties are protected from majoritarian passions by constitutional principles.[16] Classical liberalism—the Enlightenment infrastructure upon which this country was founded—accords to individuals the broadest moral authority over their own lives consistent with the maintenance of public order. So long as individuals do not act in ways that harm the persons or property of others, they are to be free of state coercion. (What constitutes harm, as I have previously noted, is the subject of considerable debate. Those holding communitarian or Puritan worldviews often argue that the existence of pornography, for example, harms society as well as individuals. At a libertarian minimum, murder, theft, vandalism, and the like are widely seen to be among the actions properly prohibited and punished by the state.) Liberalism rests upon a view of the world that separates—as many cultures do not—the public from the private. Liberal theory distinguishes between the communal and the personal; with respect to communal behaviors, it further distinguishes between public activities that are governmental, and collective actions taken through voluntary associations, which are considered private. Although the historic distinction between public and private is being substantially eroded by a number of contemporary practices, including the growth of so-called third-party government, the distinction remains a bedrock of liberal democratic theory.

Having defined spheres of human activity in this way, Enlightenment liberalism fostered a definition of justice based upon a concept of "negative" liberty, a conception that accorded great importance to liberty and individual autonomy, which were in turn defined as the right to be free of governmental constraint. The fact that economic or personal factors might operate to constrain autonomy as dramatically as any government edict was seen as unfortunate, but beside the point. The point was to limit government power.

This original understanding has been criticized as representing a cramped view of human rights. As the American population has grown, as the complexities of business and technology have created challenges that simpler societies didn't face, we have abandoned that strictly libertarian paradigm, and it no longer describes American political reality. However, the importance of negative liberty and the high priority assigned to limits on the exercise of government power continue to inform modern liberal public policy and influence public attitudes. Legislative bodies in the United States have constantly struggled against the limits imposed on government in the American system, often in pursuit of quite illiberal goals, and in other cases, in an effort to secure so-called positive or affirmative rights that were not included in the original Constitution. Civil rights is one example of rights that have been guaranteed not by the original Constitution, but by federal statutes and state statutory and constitutional provisions.

Our negative approach to the exercise of public power positions government as a neutral arbiter among citizens who are legal equals. There are many problems with such a "neutral" system, not least the fact that it does not address systemic inequalities and does not recognize the absence of a level playing field. Indeed, there are many justice issues that simply fall outside the paradigm of negative liberty as conceived by the Enlightenment's liberal state. An even more fundamental problem is that neutrality is not experienced as neutral by people who hold totalizing doctrines. For such "seamless garment" believers, no system that fails to recognize the supremacy and impose the mandates of their own value system can ever be legitimate, and we have to recognize the particular problems such individuals pose for liberal democratic systems.

Communitarians, religious conservatives, and other critics of liberalism all take issue with the most fundamental commitment of liberal democracies: that persons should be free to set and pursue their own ends, in accordance with their own values. They argue instead that political communities must insist upon a shared *telos*, a normative agreement on moral ends.[17] To those of a less authoritarian disposition, a system of government neutrality and negative rights has one overriding virtue: it makes the use of power to enforce conformity largely illegitimate.

There is a reason that Americans tend to settle even our most deeply felt differences without bloodshed—a reason we are more likely to use the courts and the political process than force to settle our disputes. (The Civil War remains a sobering reminder that this has not always been true.) An important part of that reason is that we have refused to insist on a comprehensive common moral vision enforced by the state, and have instead opted for a liberal consensus about a much more limited set of values. Basing a culture on such a "thin" consensus, however, is not tantamount to adopting a wholly procedural approach to the exercise of state authority. As I argued earlier in this chapter, a liberal democratic system does endorse ends: individual liberty and moral autonomy, equality before the law, and a high degree of tolerance for difference. Elsewhere, I have referred to the American Bill of Rights as a moral code,[18] because inherent in liberalism's hierarchy of rights and powers is a particular moral vision. Liberalism begins with respect for the value and uniqueness of each individual and requires behavior consistent with that respect, most notably equal rights for those who differ. Liberal political theory values a unity that can accommodate considerable diversity;[19] and it affirms the belief that society is strengthened and enriched by a multiplicity of voices and a constant testing of moral and political theories. It is an axiom of liberal democratic thought that allowing the state to prescribe a particular religious or moral code or to impose a significant measure of political uniformity would violate the conscience and insult the personhood of citizens. It would also engender resentments ultimately dangerous to continued social stability and civic peace.

Liberals go even further; they challenge the notion that human communities must be defined politically. They assert that political communities, in common with religious communities, ethnic groups, professional or fraternal organizations, and any number of other associations that are meaningful to their members, are all—inevitably—*partial* communities, and that their usefulness in promoting justice rests on the fact that their very existence provides maximum room for competing allegiances. Stephen Macedo has offered one of the best explanations of that thesis:

> Freedom-promoting social orders are, it appears, *pluralistic*; societies of partial allegiances in which groups endlessly

compete with each other and with the state for the allegiances of individuals, and in which individual's loyalties are divided among a variety of crosscutting (or only partially overlapping) memberships and affiliations. . . . Liberalism needs community life, therefore, and it needs community life to be constituted in a certain way. Liberal statecraft should aim for a complex, cross-cutting structure of community life in which particular group-based allegiances are tempered by other, competing group allegiances and by a state representing a common, overarching, but partial, point of view that gives everyone something in common.[20]

It is also important to recognize that, despite their reciprocal influence on each other, a society and its government are not the same thing. Governments are mechanisms for collective action, and can certainly be a venue for the expression of social values and communal aspirations, but liberals warn that there is substantial danger in reposing ultimate moral authority in a coercive state. If the goal of political community is unity without uniformity and diversity without culture war, tolerance for the divergent lifestyles and diverse values of multiple communities is both a tool *and* an end.

Liberal democrats also make another, more practical argument: there is no reasonable alternative to state neutrality, unless one wishes to use the state's coercive power to impose ends endorsed by the majority (or at least by a majority of those holding the reins of power) on unwilling minorities. John Rawls defends the liberal enterprise by positing an "overlapping consensus" of shared limited goals.[21] The complex framework he establishes rests in part on a central insight: every time you add a goal that government must enforce, you introduce a new source of conflict. In the United States today, we have deep divisions over numerous such issues.

The right to enjoy the proceeds of one's own labor conflicts with taxation that redistributes money for social ends; the right of a woman to control her own body conflicts with the religious belief of many that abortion is murder; the right of government to wage war encounters the resistance of those who believe all wars to be immoral. There are many other examples. No government can avoid such conflicts, no matter how respectful of individual autonomy, but liberal democracies are obliged to minimize them by restraining the state from intruding too much into the realms that have been defined as private. The classic formulation of this principle is that with which this section began: government intervention is warranted only when one citizen threatens harm to the person or property of another.[22] While the United States and the world's other liberal democracies have long since moderated that simple libertarian principle, often for reasons that are sound (and even more often for reasons that are specious and worrisome), I would argue that it is a formula with much to recommend it. As Marc Stier has described the liberal strategy for avoiding social conflict:

> Neutrality about the good is, for liberals, also central to their strategy for preserving internal peace. Liberals hold that we can reduce political and social conflict if we place certain matters beyond the bounds of political decision-making. Extreme and dangerous political conflict, the kind that leads to civil wars, results when governments prevent some citizens from pursuing ends of fundamental importance to them. When governments respect our rights, though, people are free to make decisions for themselves about these matters. Thus conflict about divisive issues is prevented. This strategy of avoidance is one of the prime ways in which liberals hope to keep the peace. Of course, some people may be frustrated because they cannot attain their own ends by using the power of the state to restrict what other people say and do. The liberal expectation, however, is that people

would rather have their own freedom protected than inter-
fere with the freedom of others, if only because they recognize that an illiberal regime might at some point turn against
them.[23]

The liberal democratic idea, the concept of a limited state
having a "social contract" with its citizens, was a product of
the Enlightenment. While there were certainly differences of
emphasis and disagreements on details, it was the vision that
animated the worldviews of America's founders, and it was
the basis of the American constitutional system. It reflects an
approach to morality that continues to exert enormous influence over the opinions and values of contemporary American
citizens.

Those of us who believe that liberal democratic systems are
the best—perhaps the only—way to govern radically diverse
populations have a hard job ahead of us. We must determine
how such a system can address the social and economic problems of a very complex, very diverse, very fractured modern
society while still retaining its core commitment to individual
liberty and legal equality. And that question brings us back to
Putnam's findings on trust, and the challenge those findings
pose to American government in the twenty-first century.

LIBERALISM, COMMUNITARIANISM, AND SOCIAL CAPITAL

Political theory debates can be endlessly fascinating (okay, perhaps not to everyone!), but what does any of this detour into
abstractions tell us about the real-life empirical studies of
social capital conducted by political scientists and sociologists?
What relevance do these excursions into constitutional history
and political philosophy have to the work done by Putnam and
others on diversity and distrust?

The answer lies in the nature of empirical inquiry. All research begins with a framework, a broad theoretical "lens" that shapes how scholars ask their questions and through which they analyze their data. In that sense, all questions—even the most seemingly scientific or factual—incorporate a political perspective. Barbara Arneil, a Canadian scholar, has analyzed the political theory implicit in concepts of social capital, particularly as articulated by Putnam, and has advanced one of the more intriguing critiques of that theory, a critique she has tied firmly to communitarianism:

> Social capital, as a concept, has had such a profound impact in such a short time for several reasons. First, it represents an important shift in focus, within Western political theory, away from either the state or citizen to the civic space in between. In this regard, the social capital thesis parallels two influential schools of thought within contemporary liberal democratic theory, namely communitarianism and "third way" theory. In both cases, civic space or community is the starting point of analysis, rather than either the rights-bearing citizen of liberalism or the equality-bearing state of socialism or social democracy.[24]

Arneil finds social capital theory as embraced by Coleman and Putnam to be very different from the "European school" definition associated with Pierre Bourdieu. (Bourdieu concluded that social capitalism—in common with economic capitalism—"is an ideology of inclusion and exclusion: a means by which the powerful may protect and further their interests against the less powerful.")[25] Arneil sees Putnam's formulation as an appeal for solidarity that goes well beyond the liberal democratic notion of civic participation. She identifies it with "civic republicanism"—an appeal for civic virtue and unity. Social capital, at least as Putnam has envisioned it, calls

appropriate committees in the House and Senate to "keep tabs" on the agencies, and to investigate and conduct hearings when there is evidence of a problem. And we expect the courts to hold the government responsible when its agencies operate improperly or unconstitutionally.

That oversight function has failed frequently over the past decade. And thanks to a media more pervasive and instantaneous than ever before in our history—thanks to the multitude of all-news television channels, 24/7 "news holes," blogs, and the Internet—more and more people have become aware of those failures. In response to this information, we trust less. If I can't count on the EPA to cite polluters, or on the FEC to monitor political campaign practices, or the president to tell the truth about Iran's weapons programs, I don't have private-sector options that can replace the role of the government. There are no satisfactory alternatives.

When government stops functioning at an adequate level, that failure affects us all. Ineffective oversight enables private players to break the rules; loss of government integrity allows special interests to "buy" special treatment. When we see evidence that government is abusing its power or breaking its own rules, we no longer know whom or what we can trust.

The bottom line? The color of our neighbors' skin or the odd shape of their house of worship may shake up our assumptions about their likely values or behaviors, but the real culprit (if culprits we must have) is our current profound lack of confidence in the integrity of our *institutions*. In a complex society, it is simply not possible to depend upon good will, tribal norms, or social sanctions to enforce trustworthy behavior. The kind of trust we need in order to generate the social capital required in order to make contemporary American society work requires trust in the governing institutions we have established to police governmental, corporate, and individual behavior.

Our current lack of confidence in those institutions is an understandable and eminently reasonable reaction to the accumulated evidence. Academics who study and teach public administration have identified a host of "best practices"—the sorts of behaviors and competencies that engender public trust and demonstrate the ability of institutions to do their jobs and to be responsive to the public will. Anyone who has read the newspapers or listened to broadcast or cable news—not to mention the multitude of blogs that have proliferated over the past few years—cannot help but be aware (often *painfully* aware) that something has gone very, very wrong.

If you wonder why people have become less trusting, read the next chapter.

NOTES

1. New York Historical Society, 1771.

2. J. M. Hagedorn and B. Rauch, "Variations in Urban Homicide," *City Futures Conference*, Chicago, 2004.

3. Sheila Suess Kennedy, *What's a Nice Republican Girl Like Me Doing at the ACLU?* (Amherst, NY: Prometheus Books, 1992).

4. Thomas Friedman, "Obama on the Nile," *New York Times*, June 11, 2008.

5. I say "cultural acceptance" because—although too few citizens are familiar with the explicit ideological bases of American political philosophy—most of us have been socialized into a culture with values based upon that philosophy. To quote the immortal words of Superman, most Americans really do believe in Truth, Justice and the American Way.

6. Todd Gitlin, *The Intellectuals and the Flag* (New York: Columbia University Press, 2006), p. 131.

7. Originally, of course, the limitations of the Bill of Rights applied only against the federal government, leaving state governments free to infringe the same individual liberties about which the

founders were so solicitous. Madison had wanted to apply the Bill of Rights to state and local government, but the colonies were too jealous of their prerogatives and powers—and too distrustful of the new central government—to allow that at the time. Much as slavery made the founders' ringing affirmations of human liberty ring a bit hollow, their failure to restrain state officials from engaging in the sorts of mischief that they were forbidding to their federal counterparts undercut arguments about the need to limit official power. Neither abolition of slavery nor nationalization of the Bill of Rights would become reality until passage of the Thirteenth and Fourteenth Amendments, and a bloody civil war. That said, the government of the new United States was a radical departure from other governments of its day, and its aspirations facilitated a steady movement toward an ever more expansive definition of individual liberty.

8. Hamilton proved to be all too prescient: Justice Scalia, for one, has been scornful of privacy rights for the reason that the word *privacy* does not *specifically* appear in the constitutional text.

9. How "harm to others" is to be defined is, of course, a highly contentious matter. Liberal principles are deceptively simple; their proper application (as evidenced by the thousands of books written on the topic) is anything but simple.

10. Michael Sandel, *Democracy's Discontent: America in Search of a Public Philosophy* (Cambridge, MA: Belknap Press, 1996).

11. Ibid.

12. The question of who will choose the ends, and who will define what the "right thing" is and exercise the power to enforce "right ends," is seldom addressed. Presumably, the majority will do so.

13. Ronald Beiner, "What Liberalism Means," *Social Philosophy and Policy* 13, no. 1 (1996): 190–206.

14. William Galston, *Liberal Purposes: Goods, Virtues, and Diversity in the Liberal State* (Cambridge: Cambridge University Press, 1991).

15. Ronald Dworkin, "Constitutionalism and Democracy 1," *European Journal of Philosophy* 3, no. 1 (1995): 2.

16. Fareed Zakaria, *The Future of Freedom: Illiberal Democracy at Home and Abroad* (New York: W. W. Norton & Company, 2004).

17. Stephen Mulhall and Adam Swift, *Liberalism and Communitarianism* (Oxford: Blackwell, 1992). See also Sandel, *Democracy's Discontent.*

18. Kennedy, *What's a Nice Republican Girl Like Me Doing at the ACLU?*

19. Will Kymlicka, "Social Unity in a Liberal State," *Social Philosophy and Policy* 13 (1996): 105–36.

20. Stephen Macedo, *Liberalism Citizenship, Civil Society and Civic Education* (Fale University Press, 1996), p. 255.

21. John Rawls, "The Law of Peoples," *Critical Inquiry* 20, no. 1 (1993): 36.

22. Robert Nozick, *Anarchy, State, and Utopia* (New York: Basic Books, 1974).

23. Marc Stier, "Principles and Prudence: Reconciling Liberalism and Communitarianism," paper delivered at the Annual Meeting of the American Political Science Association, August 31–September 3, 2000, Washington, DC.

24. Barbara Arneil, *Diverse Communities: The Problem with Social Capital* (Cambridge: Cambridge University Press, 2006), p. 1.

25. Ibid., p. 8.

26. Ibid., p. 7.

27. In fact, she cites several studies suggesting that greater trust leads to increased participation, rather than the other way around.

28. Robert Wuthnow and J. H. Evans, *The Quiet Hand of God: Faith-Based Activism and the Public Role of Mainline Protestantism* (Berkeley: University of California Press, 2002), p. 86.

29. Arneil, *Diverse Communities,* p. 126.

Chapter 4

GOVERNMENT

Our Institutional Infrastructure

Most arguments about politics and public policy grow out of disagreement over the proper answer to a deceptively simple question: What is the role of the state? Most of us will begin our answers to that question with the classic libertarian hypothesis about a "social contract," the conceit that free persons living in the state of nature would willingly relinquish a measure of their natural autonomy and right to self-determination in return for state-provided security. In other words, we trade the freedom to do whatever we want in return for government's promise to protect us from foreign invaders and those among our neighbors who would do us harm.

Depending upon the worldview of the person answering the question, this basic response will be supplemented in a number of very different (and often contradictory) ways. Economists will argue that a major function of government is to cure "market failure." A market failure occurs when private businesses cannot make a profit by supplying a particular good needed by the public. For example, all but the most libertarian economists will argue that in the absence of government intervention, the marketplace will not provide clean air or public parks. Many legislative battles revolve around different perspectives on what market failure is, whether it has occurred, and whether the absence of a market incentive in a given case necessarily means that government should supply the deficiency. Meanwhile, moralists on the right argue that government must protect the public from evils like pornography or prostitution; moralists on the left want the state to outlaw "hate speech" and intolerance.

Arguments for or against government action are almost always based upon fundamental disagreements over the nature and scope of government's proper role. Those arguments can be heated. They have gone on since the Revolutionary War, and given the very different worldviews we bring to the debate, they will continue on into the foreseeable future. It is interesting to note, however, that even though social scientists have produced persuasive evidence of the importance of government to the creation of social capital, and even though studies have consistently shown a relationship between governmental effectiveness and levels of social capital, very few people answer the question "What is government's job?" by replying, "to foster social capital." In this chapter, I make that case. I argue that, in a diverse society, government absolutely must provide not only physical infrastructure—the traditional airports, highways, bridges, and the like that are part of our transportation infrastructure—but also the environment that supports creation of bridging social capital equally necessary to connect citizens to each other and to the larger whole.

As we have seen, the nation's founders wrestled with how to handle a degree of diversity that seems minor now, but was radical for the times. Their goal was the creation of a single nation to which very different kinds of people (granted, at the time that meant all kinds of white men) would feel allegiance, and within which they could all function productively without having to shed their particular identities or beliefs. Their central insight was the importance of trustworthy institutions that would serve as neutral arbiters of contending religious, ethnic, and tribal interests. We need to revisit that insight, and recognize its relevance to the issue of social capital.

GOVERNMENT AND SOCIAL CAPITAL

If my thesis is correct, maintaining healthy levels of social capital requires public confidence in the trustworthiness of our commercial, social, and governmental institutions, and the trustworthiness of business and nonprofit enterprises depends upon the ability of government to play its essential role as "umpire," impartially applying and reliably enforcing the rules. The credibility and capacity of our government agencies to discharge this critical function rests on two absolutely essential elements: *accountability* and *transparency*. We have lost both over the past half century. We no longer know who is responsible for doing what, and we no longer know who is to blame when things go wrong. There are a number of reasons for this current state of affairs: some loss of transparency, for example, is a virtually inevitable result of complexity, and complexity is a virtually inevitable consequence of modern life. The field of management theory can offer insights into methods for assuring transparency and accountability in complex systems, and can help us compensate for at least some kinds of bureaucratic confusion. That said, however, I want to suggest that two major trends share substantial responsibility for getting us to our current sorry state: a lack of understanding of the importance of the distinction between public and private, especially as it relates to the operation of government; and the corruption and/or incompetence of elected officials.

In this chapter, I will take up the first of these problems, which is largely the result of well-meaning but misplaced efforts to achieve efficiency; in chapter 5, I will address the second.

Before elaborating on these explanations for the decline in social capital, it is important to acknowledge that the fact of that decline remains subject to heated debate. As we saw in chapter 1, what the data appear to confirm is a decline in levels of social trust. Nevertheless, even if—as I have argued— reciprocity is more important than trust for social capital, reciprocity requires the existence of trustworthy institutions. When government is not trustworthy, when citizens cannot rely on the Food and Drug Administration or the Social Security Administration or the Federal Emergency Management Administration, confidence declines, and social capital suffers.

REINVENTING INDIANAPOLIS: A CASE STUDY

Some government failures are ideologically driven, arguably well-intentioned efforts at "reform." In 2001, I was one of a group of Indiana scholars and public officials collaborating on a book to evaluate the just-concluded administration of Mayor Stephen Goldsmith of Indianapolis. Goldsmith had spent his two terms as chief executive deliberately creating an urban laboratory for programs designed to bring "market efficiencies" to municipal government; his stated purpose was to make government smaller and more effective, and to remove regulatory burdens on business. As we wrote in the introduction to those essays:

> During the eight years of the Goldsmith Administration, citizens of Indianapolis experienced a form of cognitive dissonance: as national media outlets waxed more and more

enthusiastic over Goldsmith's programs, local citizens became increasingly disenchanted and cynical, shrugging off the national accolades as evidence of a masterful public relations machine. For those of us who study issues of governance, the discrepancy suggested the need for a closer look at the realities of the Indianapolis experiment. Did the Goldsmith years herald new approaches to be emulated elsewhere? Or did the national coverage simply demonstrate the importance of "spin" in the treatment of urban initiatives? What really worked, what didn't, and why?[1]

Much of the investigation of what went wrong in Indianapolis—and a good deal did—has particular relevance to the question of trustworthy government and its role in creating and sustaining social capital. In particular, it illustrates the very real dangers that contracting poses for transparency and accountability—essential elements of trustworthy institutions.

Contracting out for government services is not new, and it is not necessarily a bad thing. As Donald Kettl has pointed out, however, "The constellation of issues generated by growth of government contracting spill over onto the most basic questions of American governance."[2] The growth of contracting that we have seen over the past thirty to forty years has largely been due to disenchantment with government and the belief of many theorists and politicians that privatization would be the "magic bullet" that would produce efficient and responsive government.[3] This ideological insistence on the benefits of "marketization" distinguishes it from the long-standing use of contracting as simply one useful tool among many available to the urban manager. That ideology rests largely on a view of government as primarily a provider of services for "customers" rather than a shared enterprise of citizens.[4] However, if government is more than a service provider, if it is an important generator of social capital[5] and an instrument of collective choice,[6] then any evaluation of privatization has to include an analysis of its effects on social capital. Due to the ideological fervor with which privatization was pursued, Indianapolis's experience under the Goldsmith administration presented an ideal case study from which at least tentative conclusions might be drawn.

From 1992 until 1999, his tenure as mayor of Indianapolis, Stephen Goldsmith was a leading proponent of privatization, defined as contracting out municipal services.[7] His efforts were widely reported, in glowing terms by the national media[8] and with somewhat less enthusiasm by local commentators.[9] Other public officials were urged to emulate his programs, and during his initial campaign for president, George W. Bush looked to him for domestic policy advice.[10]

For purposes of assessing the effect of privatization on accountability, public trust, and social capital formation, we looked for answers to three questions: What effect did privatization have on citizen participation and local party politics, if any? Did privatization—at least as practiced in Indianapolis— conflict with basic American constitutional principles? and How did privatization affect transparency, which is essential to public accountability?

CITIZEN PARTICIPATION

Citizens participate in their government in a number of ways beyond voting and volunteering. They serve on boards and commissions and ad hoc committees. They attend public hearings. They call city hall to complain about potholes, or to demand installation of a traffic signal. They obtain permits. They work for government, as employees or consultants or contractors. They are vendors to government agencies. In the process, they partake of a civic and political culture.

As we have seen, cultures are defined in terms of shared meanings and expectations—patterns of belief, symbols, rituals, and myths that evolve over time and function as the glue that holds associations of all kinds together.[11] Any significant change in the way government does things upsets those expectations, and requires a corresponding change in the political culture if it is to be sustainable.[12] Available literature on "reinventing government" suggests that effecting real change is anything but easy, and the way change is introduced and managed will have important policy implications. If pursued too aggressively, privatization will minimize the contacts between citizens and their government. When functions that were previously handled by government are contracted out to private companies, fewer committees and boards are needed. The number of people working for government also decreases; in Indianapolis, Goldsmith even hired private firms to dispense drainage permits. Fewer public hearings are held, because "experts" rather than citizens are driving the decision-making processes.[13] Even commercial transactions between government and its vendors diminish; government agencies are doing less and so buy fewer goods. Contracting thus substantially reduces the points of contact between citizen and city.[14] With that reduction comes an attenuation of civic ownership, a loss of the sense of shared enterprise that characterizes a workable and working polis.

Worse, at a time when so much national attention is focused on the dominance of special interests, privatization has increased the perception that most important decisions are being made by technocrats and their allies (and potential contractors) in the business community.[15] In Indianapolis, the civic leaders who had historically taken a leadership role in public life, whose motives for participation were grounded in a sense of duty rather than a potential for profit, all but disappeared. There are many reasons for that phenomenon, but privatization has been identified as one culprit. As an article in *Nuvo Newsweekly*, an Indianapolis alternative paper, noted (none too subtly):

> [T]he city has lost a class of leaders that built domes and plazas, brought in pro football and international sports. They don't make 'em like Tom Binford [a local business and civic leader] any more. Those days of community good work were replaced by Goldsmith's revolutionary urban governance that was authoritarian, cynical and sneering, with significant doses of fear and blackballing.[16]

When the public believes that important decisions are being made based on cronyism, political capital dwindles.[17] Such sentiments are difficult to measure, but their political significance is very real. Goldsmith himself attributed his decisive loss of the 1996 Indiana governor's race partly to backlash over privatization.[18]

Proponents of contracting out base their arguments largely on the presumed incapacities of government. Recommendations to privatize are thus generally accompanied by a good deal of bureaucrat-bashing and antigovernment rhetoric; certainly that was true in Indianapolis. The early days of the Goldsmith administration were marked by a procession of press releases reporting efforts to cut middle management (almost invariably referred to as "fat") and replace "bloated bureaucracy" with "more efficient" private providers of goods and services.[19] Such rhetoric devalues government and those who work for government. What is less obvious, perhaps, is that the constant denigration of government also tends to dampen enthusiasm for politics. Once your political party has elected someone to dismantle the bureaucracy, what is left to keep the political party worker engaged and interested? Political parties, after all, are about electing people to government. When government work has been demonized, it shouldn't be surprising that participation in party politics declines as well.

But privatization can have even more direct implications for party politics, as the *Howey Political Report*, an Indiana political newsletter, has documented. Just after the November 1998 elections, editor Brian Howey ran a perceptive analysis:

> When Goldsmith sacked the mid-level bureaucracy that had accumulated during the Republican Lugar and Hudnut administrations, he essentially disemboweled one of the most prolific and successful political machines of modern Midwest history. . . . Since then, the beleaguered Marion County GOP has compiled an excruciating record of failure.[20]

Howey and Schoeff went on to report the effects of that party's bloodletting: inability to get out the vote, lack of enthusiasm, and lack of manpower. As they concluded, privatization was at the root of these problems:

> Why? Because the Republican patronage is gone. The bureaucrats Goldsmith sacked don't bother to get out the vote. Unions can reward their activists, so they turn out the vote. There are no rewards for Republican partisans in Indianapolis.[21]

This lack of rewards for grassroots political activity was a key element in the politics of Indianapolis during Goldsmith's administration. While some people participate in the political process for the sheer love of it, in my younger days, at least, most party workers knew that victory would bring them *something*: maybe a city job, maybe a paved street, maybe just improved access to the powers that be. In the privatized city, what was rewarded were political contributions, not party activities like polling and registration and working the phone banks. The Goldsmith administration awarded significant contracts to private companies to manage operations that had previously been handled by municipal employees. That practice gave rise to persistent accusations that political contributors were being rewarded with lucrative city business, and fed a growing perception that privatization was simply a less-desirable form of patronage. In July 1996, the *Indianapolis Star* ran a story typical of many during Goldsmith's terms:

> Seventeen days after getting a lucrative city contract, executives of the [privately owned] Indianapolis Water Company and its development partner will throw a fundraiser for Mayor Stephen Goldsmith. . . . The $250-per-person dinner planned for Wednesday would not be the first fundraiser for Goldsmith, the Republican nominee for Governor, to come on the heels of a privatization contract.[22]

Such stories do not increase citizens' trust in their public officials, or in the conduct of the public's business, and they don't encourage citizens to participate in the political process. Where once blue-collar workers had polled their neighborhoods hoping for a job, during the Goldsmith administration, business owners hoping for a contract contributed to the mayor's reelection campaign. And nobody polled the neighborhood.

CONSTITUTIONAL ISSUES

Too many public administrators see the Constitution as a problem to be avoided rather than as a basis for legitimacy of government action. The founders devised a system of checks and balances intended to impede the efficiency of the state in order to protect individual liberty. When public administrators are concentrating on making the trains run on time (or intent upon using "interrogation techniques" that violate the Constitution), those checks can seem onerous:

Constitutional checks on power . . . provide a system of multiple veto points in the political process. These veto points limit the ability of any particular group of political leaders to simply impose its will on others in the political process. As a result, constitutional checks on power force political leaders to take account of information and opinions held by others about the effects of public policies.[23]

Some of the most consistent public criticisms of Goldsmith's reinvention efforts were focused upon the widespread perception that public decisions were made without the benefit of this constitutionally required deliberative process. This perception created an atmosphere of political cynicism that was largely absent during prior Republican administrations and that actually made it much more difficult for Goldsmith to achieve his policy objectives. In his book, *The 21st Century City*, he complains that efforts at redeveloping a portion of the riverfront were met with accusations of cronyism and hidden agendas.[24] What he clearly failed to understand was that such suspicions are an inevitable outgrowth of privatization, which gives high priority to *product* and short shrift to *process*. But it is process that creates social capital, and the openness of that process develops trust. The problem is intimately connected to the issues of political and fiscal accountability addressed below.

Only the government can violate one's civil liberties—the Bill of Rights is a list of things that the *government* is forbidden to do. Those prohibitions don't apply to private citizens. This is called the *state action doctrine*, and privatization raises troubling questions about whether and when independent contractors, even those operating under government contracts, are exercising state action so as to be bound by the Bill of Rights. Can a city avoid compliance with due process, or intentionally infringe citizens' First Amendment rights, by the simple expedient of contracting to have a private company act on the city's behalf, or do the city's work? Are records maintained by such private contractors subject to Freedom of Information inquiry? Emerging law in this area is unclear, to put it mildly. If city governments can avoid compliance with the Bill of Rights by engaging private contractors to manage selected pieces of the civic enterprise, the constitutional and political implications will be profound.

In "The End of the Republican Era," Theodore Lowi wrote that we are in danger of losing the constituency for the rule of law, preferring *authority* to *rules*.[25] While privatization is almost always defended as a method for producing smaller and more responsive government, in fact it simply empowers—*authorizes*—private interests to act under government's imprimatur. It privileges authority over the rule of law. In Indianapolis, when the private managers of the Indianapolis Wastewater Treatment Plant were charged with various improprieties, including evasion of Indiana's long-standing bid laws, Goldsmith defended the noncompliance and criticized the laws as "inadequate to the governance of a Twenty-first Century City."[26]

IMPLICATIONS FOR SOCIAL CAPITAL

One of the challenges public administrators face is managing change so that citizens experience continuity rather than dislocation. This isn't a new problem: James Madison observed that "it poisons the blessings of liberty itself [if the laws] undergo such incessant changes that no man who knows what the law is today can guess what it will be tomorrow."[27] It isn't only laws that can change; executives have broad discretion to make changes in the way government agencies are run. But even necessary change can be problematic, because stability

ical party difficulties described above. While it is easy to blame this state of affairs on Mayor Goldsmith—and certainly his management style is responsible for part of it—privatization ideology *requires* that change be a goal. How else do we understand the concept of "reinvention"? (Ironically, after all of the energy that was expended on changing the way the city did business, Hennessey's analysis proved prescient; when Goldsmith left city hall, most of his "innovations" quietly died.)

The lack of employee ownership of the new ways of doing things was only one of the problems involving personnel. Over time, one of the more important—if unappreciated—ways in which government has built bridges between citizens of different backgrounds and ethnicities has been by acting as the employer of "first resort." This has been especially true for women and minorities, easing their transition into the workforce and offering an avenue to management experience. Under Goldsmith's privatization effort, the city workforce was trimmed by 629 employees, whose functions were largely contracted out.[32] The impression in the Indianapolis African American community was that this process disproportionately affected blacks. Employment figures do show a more substantial decline in the number of African Americans employed by the civil city (i.e., employment exclusive of police and fire uniformed personnel) than among white workers. At the beginning of 1992, there were 690 African Americans employed by the city of Indianapolis; at the end of 1998, there were 460, a reduction of 230 jobs, or 33 percent. During that same period, total city employment decreased by 27 percent.

While the city gave major contracts to at least one black-owned business—Oscar Robertson Smoot, based in Ohio—the local black community viewed privatization as a method of rewarding mostly white political contributors at the expense of the blacks who had been well represented in city hall during the Hudnut administration. This perception, coupled with persistent community relations problems in the Indianapolis Police Department, had a significant negative effect on race relations in Indianapolis. As Rozelle Boyd, the then minority leader of the City-County Council, observed:

> To its own detriment, the administration was very slow to respond to the broadly publicized "Meridian Street Brawl." The Brawl was a downtown police-initiated confrontation with citizens, characterized by racial slurs, that has come to be viewed as a kind of index to the administration's general responsiveness to the minority community. This obtains in both civil and economic arenas, especially the so-called "privatization" process.[33]

The accountability issues raised by privatization are different from the sorts of issues that arise when government is providing services directly. That is partly because much of what passes for bureaucratic and governmental inefficiency is really what Russell Hardin has tactfully called "institutional design that encapsulates the self-interest of government officials,"[34] and what others call precautions against corruption. If, as many social scientists assert, trust in government requires accountability, lack of accountability contributes to distrust and cynicism about government and those who are engaged in it.

In the private sector, the market provides very effective checks and balances, as anyone who has ever gone out of business can attest. The checks and balances applied to government, however, address fundamentally different concerns. Our political system requires structural safeguards that recognize the differences between government and private enterprise, that compensate for deficiencies in leadership and protect against abuse. One of the problems with the political rhetoric accompanying privatization is its failure to acknowledge that government is fundamentally different from the private sector.

issuance of a certificate of substantial completion, contracts awarded despite the fact that fewer than the required three bids were received, and even mathematical errors in the computation of city payments due.[45]

Not surprisingly, by the end of Goldsmith's administration, questions about fiscal management and financial accountability were constant.[46] Rather than reinventing city government, critics were suggesting that what Goldsmith had really "reinvented" were two questionable and decidedly old-fashioned political behaviors: patronage, and the art of concealing and postponing costs until subsequent administrations took office. And needless to say, Indianapolis residents had come to be highly suspicious of their municipal government.

THE HOLLOW STATE[47]

Privatization doesn't just reduce public trust in government. There is another aspect of contracting out that arguably affects the formation of social capital, and that is the changes that public-private partnerships produce in the organizations with which government agencies contract, especially nonprofit organizations. Interestingly, despite a widespread belief among nonprofit scholars that the voluntary sector is an important generator of social capital, few researchers have addressed the question whether the seemingly inexorable growth of government contracting with nonprofit organizations might be contributing to, slowing, or changing the character of the social capital that these organizations produce. (On the other hand, none to my knowledge have investigated whether contracting out reduces government's own ability to generate social capital.)

Sociologists and political scientists have, however, recognized the importance of the nonprofit sector as a generator of social capital. As one research team has put it:

Our basic argument is that nonprofit organizations are an important part of local social networks that connect individuals and organizations within a community. These social networks are critical to the development of local community capacity to solve social problems, support individuals, and mobilize residents for collective action.[48]

Backman and Smith also note the somewhat circular nature of social capital creation, noting, "In short, social support at the community level is a product of social capital, which is itself a product of the broader social networks in a community."[49] Nonprofits have an important place in those "broader social networks." As Robert Wuthnow has noted, "Nonprofits may be more capable than government or market organizations of generating social norms of trust, cooperation and mutual support due to their noncoercive character and appeals to charitable and social motives."[50] Other researchers have noted the important role of nonprofit organizations such as neighborhood and community associations, sports clubs, and cultural organizations in generating social capital. While it is clear that not all associations contribute to social capital in the same way or to the same degree,[51] it is equally clear that the role of the voluntary sector in the production of social capital is extremely important, and that production and maintenance of social capital is in turn critical to the health of democratic processes.

Voluntary organizations—nonprofits and NGOs—act as a buffer between the state and the individual citizen. The so-called third sector, composed of voluntary associations, is something other than the family unit, with its unique kinship relationships, or government, with its monopoly on the legitimate exercise of coercive power. The networks of trust and reciprocity developed through participation in voluntary organizations are neither governmental nor individual; instead, these nonprofit organizations are often described as "mediating institutions," facilitating and moderating the relationships between citizens and their formal governmental structures. As the points of contact and potential conflict between individuals and the modern administrative state increase,[52] the importance of such mediating institutions, and the networks created by and through them, increases as well.

The continued health of the voluntary sector is as important to democratic governments as it is to the individual citizens it serves. The nonprofit sector is where citizens acquire human capital, those skills needed for effective community participation, and it is the arena in which they build social capital—the connections that enable them to use those skills in concert with others to influence political and community decision making. The networks of trust and reciprocity generated by nonprofit activity are resources from which government draws personnel, paid and voluntary, and to which it increasingly looks for program implementation. Especially in an era of privatization (defined as the delivery of government services through nonprofit and for-profit intermediaries), the ability of government contractors to deliver social services depends to a considerable degree upon the adequacy of their networks—or to put it another way, upon the extent of their social capital. If that is the case, however, we need to ask a question: What if the increasing use of nonprofit agencies to deliver government services is changing the character of those agencies in a way that is eroding their ability to generate social capital?

A number of studies have found that increases in commercial activity by nonprofits tended to alter the role of board members, as the organizations became less dependent upon the financial contributions by the members of their boards. Similar concerns have been raised by the increasing dependence of nonprofits on government contracts, which in the United States now account for nearly 40 percent of all voluntary sector income (and, by some estimates, 80 percent of the income of social service–providing nonprofits). In an important book published in 1993, *Nonprofits for Hire: The Welfare State in the Age of Contracting*, Steven Rathgeb Smith and Michael Lipsky were among the first to explore a number of the issues raised for government and the nonprofit sector by virtue of the increasing reliance of the latter upon government contracts. Scholarship since that time has served to amplify those concerns:

> American social policy is in the midst of a dramatic restructuring of the way public social services are provided. Although government funding of nonprofit service organizations dates to the colonial period, only in the last 25 years did this government-nonprofit strategy emerge as a widespread and favored tool of public service delivery. But entrusting the most vulnerable citizens and the most delicate service tasks to private agencies is not simply a matter of choice between "making" or "buying" services. This might be the case when one considers contracting out for pencils, computer services, or strategic weapons. But when it comes to purchasing the care and control of drug addicts, the safety and nurturing of children, the relief of hunger and the regulation of family life (through child protective activities) from private agencies, other values than efficiency are at stake. We contend that the impact of this transformation on the future of the American welfare state has not received adequate attention.[53]

We are beginning to see the contours of that transformation and its effect upon the voluntary sector. Significant attention has been paid to the management and contracting challenges posed by privatized service delivery methods,[54] and (in the United States) to the implications for the doctrine of state action and constitutional accountability.[55] However, other effects of this governance shift have been less fully explored.

For example, there has been little or no scholarship investigating whether participation in government itself, by serving on boards and commissions, ad hoc committees, and the like, facilitates the production of social capital, although it seems likely that such activities create bridging social capital. Participation in such government activities is likely to bring a citizen into contact with persons he otherwise might not meet, and the common experience of service has the potential, at least, of generating trust and reciprocity. As we saw in the Indianapolis experience, as government outsources more and more functions, it relies less on such boards and commissions and more on the "experts" who hold the relevant contracts. Citizens are increasingly excluded from civic activity and arenas for democratic deliberation. It isn't much of a stretch to conclude that this exclusion may affect production of social capital.

A related question has begun to generate research interest, however, and that is the question of the effect of these contracting relationships on the nonprofit partner, or contractor. When nonprofit organizations contract with government agencies to provide services, they become accountable in ways that are qualitatively different from the accountability owed to board members and even donors. Governments (quite properly) require fiscal and programmatic reporting, evidence of minimum financial management standards, and a level of professionalism in the delivery of services. Overall, such requirements may well improve the efficiency and management practices of the nonprofit involved. (Lester Salomon, among others, has written about the amateurism of the nonprofit sector, and has contrasted that amateurism with the professionalism of public and private agencies.)[56] The unanswered question is whether the more businesslike, more streamlined, more professionalized organizations that emerge as a result of these public-private partnerships are still able to provide the benefits—including the creation of social capital—that truly voluntary associations afford, and if so, whether and how the nature of those benefits changes. A 1997 GAO report, for example, linked the growing dependence by American nonprofits on government contracting to a reduction in grassroots education efforts by such organizations.[57] Sundeep Aulakh has reported a similar phenomenon in Great Britain, suggesting that

> as voluntary agencies take on the state's delivery functions, their defining qualities such as encouraging community development and participation are threatened. Ultimately, it has been argued that as voluntary agencies have increasingly taken on the state's delivery functions (and as the state influences their management) they have become agents of the state.[58]

Other studies have noted a decrease in volunteer and donor involvement in the conduct of the business of such organizations.[59] This raises a troubling question: Is there a point at which a nonprofit or NGO loses its identity as a voluntary organization and becomes simply a differently constituted arm of the state? If so, what happens to the role of the nonprofit in producing social capital?

As we have seen in the Indianapolis example, many of the most severe criticisms of government contracting revolve around questions of accountability.[60] If government transparency and accountability are being compromised by the growth of contracting out, one potential consequence is increased citizen distrust of government agencies. As we will see in chapter 5, widely reported evidence of cronyism, corruption, and the politicizing of the federal contracting process has contributed to widespread cynicism about government in general.

There is also a well-founded, but far less obvious concern that these contractual arrangements may be stifling the kinds of grassroots advocacy efforts that have typically characterized private, voluntary organizations and even some for-profit contractors.[61] In democratic systems, citizenship implies participation in democratic deliberation; indeed, to the extent that social capital is valued, it is in large part because it is thought to facilitate that participation. Putnam, among others, considers political participation to be an indicator of the presence or absence of social capital. If contracting depresses such activities in the nonprofit sector, it only makes sense to ask whether one consequence is to reduce social capital.

Studies suggest that when nonprofits or NGOs enter into contracts with government agencies, decision making within the contracting organization tends to shift from the board of directors to the executive director.[62] Staff tends to grow as well, crowding out volunteers in favor of paid personnel who are hired and fired by the executive director. This is understandable; if my organization has a contractual obligation to provide a service, reliance on volunteers to perform under the contract poses a number of risks. However, if social capital grows out of collective action and decision making, the shift to individual authority and away from collective deliberation by boards and volunteers is worrisome. Similarly, when nonprofits become financially dependent upon government contracts, much decision making shifts from the voluntary association to the government. That further diminishes opportunities for democratic deliberation. Government typically tells its contractors what services to deliver, what clients to serve, what services those clients should receive, and which clients should be given priority. (Again, it must be emphasized that this is entirely appropriate—government agencies are spending tax dollars and have a responsibility to ensure that those dollars are properly spent.) But the result is that decisions previously made in a collective fashion by volunteers and board members are now made by government. Smith gives an example: a nonprofit organization located in Seattle provides an array of programs for immigrants, with a special emphasis on housing construction and renovation, and economic development.[63] The organization relies upon government contracts for a significant percentage of its income, and the money comes subject to a number of conditions and extensive monitoring. Board members complain that they have lost control over their programming, and decision making has shifted from broad policy matters to questions about how to implement government directives. Such a shift would certainly seem to have negative implications for democratic deliberation and social capital.

Finally, government financial support of nonprofits can crowd out private donations.[64] To the extent that the act of charitable giving is *itself* a generator of interest and involvement in the broader community, we have to wonder whether this consequence of contracting might also suppress formation of social capital.

I will be the first to admit that these are hypothesized consequences, and that a good deal of research on these questions remains to be done. Furthermore, some of the outcomes suggested by the scholarship are conflicting: on the one hand, we are warned that contracting out has shifted decision making from government to less accountable voluntary organizations; on the other hand, concerns are raised about contractual constraints that reduce nonprofit decision making. It is unlikely that both results are true. It is also possible to argue that government contracting may bring more citizens into contact with democratic policy processes, may enlarge and extend the networks of which they are members, and thus may increase, rather than diminish, social capital formation. Too, the foregoing discussion ignores the wide variety of the nonprofit sector, and the substantial differences between nonprofit organizations. Service-providing organizations may have very different experiences with contracting than other types of nonprofits; indeed, the nature of the service may change the nature of the experience. Nonprofits that contract with local government units may have a different experience than those doing business with the federal government. Finally, the question as I have framed it ignores the very real likelihood that some nonprofit organizations encourage bonding, rather than bridging social capital, and are actually inimical to democratic processes.

There are disquieting indications that contracting produces what Milward has called a "hollow state," depriving government agencies of institutional capacity and complicating efforts to ensure accountability.[65] If contracting is also "hollowing out" nonprofit organizations—an essential component of civil society—that possibility deserves attention and study. Even if the picture is more mixed—if some contracting arrangements are actually beneficial to social capital formation, while others are not—we need to be able to distinguish between them, and curtail those practices that are detrimental to civic trust. The one thing that seems clear is that contracting is changing the nature of the voluntary sector, and we need to know which of those changes are supportive of democratic processes and which are inimical to them.

THE MEANING OF IT ALL

Privatization is a classic example of unintended consequences. No public official called a meeting to figure out what new approach to service delivery might diminish social capital. Furthermore, as research has raised doubts about the economic benefits and management challenges of such arrangements, enthusiasm for privatization has abated. Like many other management fads, it is likely that contracting out will once again be viewed as one option among many others for providing public services, and will be used more appropriately and judiciously.

Furthermore, privatization has been at most a contributor to the problem. It has not been an insignificant factor, but neither has it been the major culprit. For a discussion of the most serious problem with government's trustworthiness, we must turn to chapter 5.

NOTES

1. Ingrid Ritchie and Sheila Suess Kennedy, eds., *To Market, to Market: Reinventing Indianapolis* (Lanham, MD: University Press of America, 2001).

2. Donald F. Kettl, *Sharing Power: Public Governance and Private Markets* (Washington, DC: Brookings Institution Press, 1993), p. 211.

3. Stephen Goldsmith, "Moving Municipal Services into the Marketplace," *Carnegie Council Privatization Project*, no. 14 (New York, November 20, 1992). David Boaz, *Libertarianism: A Primer* (New York: Free Press, 1997). R. A. Epstein, *Simple Rules for a Complex World* (Cambridge, MA: Harvard University Press, 1995).

4. John J. Kirlin, "What Government Must Do Well: Creating Value for Society," *Journal of Public Administration Research and Theory* (1996): 161–85.

5. Van Romine, *Civic Participation, Social Capital and Leadership* (La Jolla Institute, 1998). William Hudnut, *Cities on the Rebound: A Vision for Urban America* (Washington, DC: Urban Land Institute, 1998).

6. Kirlin, "What Government Must Do Well," p. 161.

7. Technically, privatization is what Margaret Thatcher did in Great Britain; it involves selling off government enterprises to the private sector, where they are owned, managed, and pay taxes like any other private business. In the United States, privatization generally means that the government is providing goods or services through a third-party contractor. In these arrangements, the government dictates the nature of the service, the identities of the recipi-

ents, and usually the method of delivery. And the government still pays the bill.

8. "A Mayor Shows Gore's Team the Way," *Washington Post*, August 25, 1993. William Stern, "We Got Real Efficient Real Quick," *Forbes*, June 20, 1994.

9. Jack Miller in *To Market, to Market: Reinventing Indianapolis*, ed. Ingrid Ritchie and Sheila Suess Kennedy (Lanham, MD: University Press of America, 2001). Brian A. Howey, "Peeling the Goldsmith Onion: The Mayor Brought Dramatic Changes to City Government, but What It Cost and What We Got Is a Mystery," *NUVO Newsweekly*, December 30, 1998. Howey, "Are Goldsmith's Books Crooked?" *NUVO Newsweekly*, January 14, 1999. Howey, "Goldsmith's Community Credit Card," *NUVO Newsweekly*, May 20, 1999.

10. Martha Brant, "The Sage of Indianapolis," *Newsweek Magazine*, January 3, 2000.

11. J. Thomas Hennessey Jr., "Reinventing Government: Does Leadership Make the Difference?" *Public Administration Review* 58 (1998): 525.

12. William Blomquist, interview with the author, January 23, 1999. R. J. Gregory, "Social Capital Theory and Administrative Reform: Maintaining Ethical Probity in Public Service," *Public Administration Review* 59 (1999): 63–75.

13. W. Montgomery and Sam Nunn, "Privatization, Participation, and the Planning Process: A Case Study of Wastewater Treatment Infrastructure," *Public Works Management and Policy* 1 (1996): 43–59. Daniel Yankelovich, *Coming to Public Judgment: Making Democracy Work in a Complex World* (Syracuse, NY: Syracuse University Press, 1991).

14. Stephen Rathgeb Smith and Michael Lipsky, *Nonprofits for Hire: The Welfare State in the Age of Contracting* (Cambridge, MA: Harvard University Press, 1993).

15. Yankelovich, *Coming to Public Judgment*, p. 241.

16. Harrison Ullmann, "Revolution: A City Where the People Are the Problem," *NUVO Newsweekly*, May 27, 1998.

17. R. J. Gregory, "Social Capital Theory and Administrative

Reform: Maintaining Ethical Probity in Public Service," *Public Administration Review* 59, no. 1 (1999): 65.

18. D. L. Haase, "Goldsmith Says City Innovation Has Its Price," *Indianapolis Star*, December 4, 1996, p. C1.

19. David Remondini, "Goldsmith Looking to Cut City Force by Twenty-five Percent," *Indianapolis Star*, November 26, 1991.

20. Brian Howey and M. Schoeff Jr., "Inside the Stunning '98 Indiana Election," *Howey Political Report*, November 1998.

21. Ibid.

22. K. Johnston, "Critics Question the Propriety of Fundraiser for Goldsmith," *Indianapolis Star*, July 14, 1996.

23. M. W. Spicer, *The Founders, the Constitution, and Public Administration: A Conflict in Worldviews* (Washington, DC: Georgetown University Press, 1995), p. 51.

24. Stephen Goldsmith, *The 21st Century City* (Washington, DC: Regnery Publishing, 1997).

25. Theodore Lowi, *The End of the Republican Era* (Norman: University of Oklahoma Press, 1995).

26. "Privatization Run Amuck," *Indianapolis Star*, August 30, 1994.

27. Spicer, *The Founders*, p. 47.

28. William Blomquist, interview with the author, January 23, 1999.

29. Hennessey Jr., "Reinventing Government: Does Leadership Make the Difference?" p. 522.

30. Miller, in *To Market, to Market*.

31. Beth O'Laughlin, interview with the author, June 28, 2000.

32. Kevin Morgan, "Family Feud: Hudnut Raps Goldsmith," *Indianapolis Star*, November 25, 1993.

33. Rozelle Boyd, interview with the author, February 8, 1999.

34. Russell Hardin, "In Trust and Governance," in *Trust and Governance*, ed. V. Braithwaite and M. Levi, 12 (New York: Russell Sage Foundation, 1998).

35. Jane Jacobs, *Systems of Survival: A Dialogue on the Moral Foundations of Commerce and Politics* (New York: Random House, 1992).

36. D. H. Rosenbloom, James D. Carroll, and Jonathan D. Car-

roll, *Constitutional Competence for Public Managers: Cases and Commentary* (Itasca, IL: FE Peacock Publishers, 2000).

37. R. J. Gregory, "Social Capital Theory and Administrative Reform: Maintaining Ethical Probity in Public Service," *Public Administration Review* 59, no. 1 (1999): 66.

38. John Krull, interview with the author. January 27, 1999. Harrison Ullmann, interview with the author, January 23, 1999.

39. Howey, "Peeling the Goldsmith Onion." Howey, "Are Goldsmith's Books Crooked?" Howey, "Goldsmith's Community Credit Card."

40. Kettl, *Sharing Power.*

41. Miller, in *To Market, to Market.*

42. Howey, "Are Goldsmith's Books Crooked?"

43. Ibid.

44. Kathy Davis, interview with the author, May 23, 2000.

45. State Board of Accounts, "Special Report of Construction Projects for Municipal Gardens Recreation Center and Carson Park Recreation Center," September 16, 1999. State Board of Accounts, "Special Report of Construction Projects for Franklin-Edgewood Park, Krannert-King-Brookside Aquatic Centers, and Perry Park Ice Rink and Aquatic Facility," September 16, 1999.

46. Howey, "Are Goldsmith's Books Crooked?" "Debt Load for City Is Becoming a Key Issue," *Indianapolis Star*, June 29, 1999. Brian Williams, "Our Fiscal Future Will Be Challenge for Next Mayor," *Indianapolis Business Journal*, November 1–7, 1999.

47. The term *hollow state* was first coined by Brinton Milward. See Howard B. Milward, "Nonprofit Contracting and the Hollow State," *Public Administration Review* 54, no. 1 (January/February 1994): 73.

48. E. V. Backman and S. R. Smith, "Healthy Organizations, Unhealthy Communities?" *Nonprofit Management and Leadership* 10, no. 4 (2000): 356.

49. Ibid., p. 358.

50. Robert Wuthnow, H. K. Anheier, and J. Boli, *Between States and Markets: The Voluntary Sector in Comparative Perspective* (Princeton, NJ: Princeton University Press, 1991).

51. D. Stolle and T. R. Rochon, "Are All Associations Alike?" *Beyond Tocqueville: Civil Society and the Social Capital Debate in Comparative Perspective* (2001): 143–56. Backman and Smith, "Healthy Organizations, Unhealthy Communities?"

52. The growth of government in Western industrialized countries has multiplied enormously the points of contact between citizens and their governments. Obtaining Social Security benefits, getting a drivers license, applying for a student loan, and numerous other day-to-day transactions involve government at some level.

53. Stephen Rathgeb Smith and Michael Lipsky, *Nonprofits for Hire: The Welfare State in the Age of Contracting* (Cambridge, MA: Harvard University Press, 1993).

54. Sheila Suess Kennedy and Wolfgang Bielefeld, "Government Shekels without Government Shackles? The Administrative Challenges of Charitable Choice," *Public Administration Review* 61, no. 1 (2002). Ellen Dannin, "To Market, to Market: Caveat Emptor," in *To Market, to Market: Reinventing Indianapolis*, ed. Ingrid Ritchie and Sheila Suess Kennedy, 1–55 (Lanham, MD: University Press of America, 2001). Government Accountability Office report, 1997.

55. Sheila Suess Kennedy, "Accountability: The Achilles Heel," in *To Market, to Market: Reinventing Indianapolis*, ed. Ingrid Richie and Sheila Suess Kennedy (Lanham, MD, University Press of America, 2001).

56. Salamon proposes a theory of "voluntary failure" (pp. 111–13), akin to the theory of market failure. He posits that the voluntary sector is the preferred mechanism for providing collective goods, and that government is a residual institution needed because of certain shortcomings of the voluntary sector. These shortcomings include: 1) Philanthropic insufficiency, defined as a lack of a reliable stream of resources sufficient to respond to social needs; 2) Philanthropic particularism, defined as a focus on particular subgroups. This is sometimes considered a strength of the sector; however, some subgroups may not be favored by those with resources. This also can lead to duplication of services, when each subgroup wants its own agencies; 3) Philanthropic paternalism, when those with the greatest resources get to define community needs and decide how they are to be met; and 4) Philanthropic amateurism, in part due to paternalism, where the understanding of

and care for the needy is entrusted to well-meaning amateurs and those with moral agendas, rather than to professionals trained to deal with the issues. Salamon suggests that the philanthropic sector's weaknesses correspond to the public sector's strengths, so that partnerships work to the benefit of both. Government can deal with the issues of sufficiency, particularism, paternalism, and professionalism, while the non-profit sector can personalize service provision, adjust care to needs of clients, and provide competition. See Lester M. Salamon, "Partners in Public Service: The Scope and Theory of Government-Nonprofit Relations," *Nonprofit Sector: A Research Handbook* (1987): 99–117.

57. Government Accountability Office report, 1997.

58. Sundeep Aulakh, "The Transformation of the UK State: Rolling Back or Rolling Out?" paper presented at the Transatlantic Policy Consortium Conference, Speyer, Germany, 2003.

59. Arthur C. Brooks, "Is There a Dark Side to Government Support for Nonprofits?" *Public Administration Review* 60, no. 3 (2000): 211–18.

60. Dannin, "To Market, to Market: Caveat Emptor," pp. 1–55.

61. Government Accountability Office report, 1997. Matthew A. Crenson and Benjamin Ginsberg, *Downsizing Democracy: How America Sidelined Its Citizens and Privatized Its Public* (Baltimore: Johns Hopkins University Press, 2002). Marilyn Gittell, *Limits to Citizen Participation* (Beverly Hills, CA: Sage Publications, 1980).

62. Smith and Lipsky, *Nonprofits for Hire.*

63. Stephen Rathgeb Smith, "Government Financing of Nonprofit Activity," in *Nonprofits and Government: Collaboration and Conflict*, ed. Elizabeth T. Boris and C. Eugene Steurle, 198 (Washington, DC: Urban Institute Press, 1999).

64. Arthur Brooks, "Is There a Dark Side to Government Support for Nonprofits?" *Public Administration Review* 60, no. 3 (2000): 211–18.

65. Milward, "Nonprofit Contracting and the Hollow State." p. 73.

Chapter 5

BETRAYAL OF TRUST

The past decade has produced an unremitting—and seemingly escalating—litany of unsettling news, emanating from virtually all the major sectors of American society. It sometimes seems as if each day brings a new challenge or scandal. We sustained a stunning attack on American soil, reminding us that the oceans no longer safeguard us from the hostility of others. We invaded another nation because we were told it had weapons of mass destruction that made it an imminent threat, only to discover that no such weapons existed. News reports have brought daily warnings that our governing institutions are "off the track." There has been visible, worrying erosion of our constitutional safeguards. Meanwhile, the imperatives of population growth and commerce, technology and transportation, as well as politics, have eroded local control and hollowed out "states' rights," leaving people powerless to change or even affect many aspects of their legal and political environments.

Old-fashioned corruption and greed have combined with political and regulatory dysfunction to undermine business ethics. Enron, WorldCom, Halliburton, the subprime housing market meltdown and the subsequent financial collapse it triggered—these and so many others are the stuff of daily news reports. Newspapers report on the stratospheric salaries of corporate CEOs, often in articles running alongside stories about the latest layoffs, reductions in employer-funded healthcare, and loss of pensions for thousands of retired workers. Throughout most of this time, business forecasters have insisted that the economy was in great shape—a pronouncement that met with disbelief from wage earners who hadn't participated in any of the reported economic gains, and whose take-home pay in real terms had often declined. By 2007, the gap between rich and poor Americans was as wide as it had been in the 1920s.[1] Many of the business scandals were tied to failures by—or incompetence of—federal regulatory agencies; others were traced back to K Street influence peddlers, of whom Jack Abramoff is only the most prominent example.[2]

Meanwhile, American religious institutions have not exactly covered themselves with glory, heavenly or otherwise. Doctrinal battles over ordination of women and gays have split congregations. Revelations ranging from misappropriation of funds to protection of pedophiles to the "outing" of stridently antigay clergy have discouraged believers and increased skepticism of organized religion. In that other American religion, major league sports, the news has been no better. High-profile investigations confirmed widespread use of steroids by baseball players. At least one NBA referee was found guilty of taking bribes to "shade" close calls, and others have been accused of betting on games at which they officiate. Football players seem habitually prone to wind up on the front pages;

Atlanta Falcon Michael Vick's federal indictment and guilty plea on charges related to dog fighting was tabloid fodder for several weeks. Even charitable organizations have come under fire: a few years ago, United Way of America had to fire an executive director accused of using contributions to finance a lavish lifestyle. Other charities have been accused of spending far more on overhead than on good works.

The constant drumbeat of scandal has played out against a background of gridlock and hyperpartisanship in Washington. And—more significantly, for purposes of the public mood—all of it has been endlessly recycled and debated by a newly pervasive media: all-news channels that operate twenty-four hours a day, talk radio, satellite radio, "alternative" newspapers, and literally millions of blogs, in addition to the more traditional media outlets.[3] Political gaffes and irreverent commentaries find their way to YouTube, where they are viewed by millions; wildly popular political satirists like Jon Stewart, Bill Maher, and Stephen Colbert have used cable television to engage a generational cohort that had not traditionally focused on political news. Everyone who leaves government service seems to write at least one book pointing an accusing finger or otherwise raising an alarm; their exposés join literally hundreds of other books (most of them alarmist) cranked out by pundits, political scientists, and scolds playing to partisan passions. The political maneuvering, cozy cronyism, and policy trade-offs that used to be the stuff of "inside baseball," of interest only to political players and policy wonks, are increasingly the stuff of everyday conversation at the local Starbucks. In this hyperheated media environment, if you don't like the news, you can run—but you really can't hide. Even partisans who limit their news sources to those likely to validate their opinions hear about the latest controversies, if only from their chosen perspective.

When you add to this constant din of revelations, charges, and countercharges, the highly visible and widely reported ineptitude of the Bush administration's handling of Hurricane Katrina; the drawn-out, inconclusive war in Iraq; the even more nebulous and worrisome conduct of the so-called War on Terror; and mounting questions about the nature and extent of government surveillance, is it any wonder American citizens have grown cynical? Furthermore, all these miscues and misdeeds—and many more—are taking place in an environment characterized by economic uncertainty and polarization, as well as accelerating social, technological, and cultural change (including but certainly not limited to the growth of diversity). Add in the so-called culture wars, and it's not hard to understand why generalized trust has eroded. In fact, the better question might be why we haven't had *more* social unrest and *more* generalized distrust.

BETWEEN THEN AND NOW

One would have to be either dishonest or naive to suggest that all was good and honorable in American government until the Bush administration. A cursory glance through even relatively recent history will uncover plenty of unsavory behaviors, and for an example of social upheaval it would be difficult to top the Civil War. But for purposes of analyzing our current disaffection with our governing institutions, it is probably sufficient to begin with the disruptions of the 1960s. "The Sixties" has come to be shorthand for the period between 1956 and 1974, a period that encompassed the civil rights movement, the first stirrings of the women's movement, along with the Vietnam War and the student protests triggered by that conflict. The Sixties saw the emergence of the Chicano movement, the New Left, and radical organizations like the Weathermen and Students for a Democratic Society (SDS). The assassinations of John F. Kennedy, Martin Luther King Jr., and Bobby

Kennedy were traumatic events, as were the urban riots that followed Dr. King's assassination. George Wallace ran for president as a third-party candidate; his slogan was "Segregation now, segregation tomorrow, segregation forever." The 1968 Democratic National Convention in Chicago turned into a police riot, and Americans were riveted to their television screens as cameras panned over police officers clubbing young protestors and dragging them to jail.

Conflict and unrest were not restricted to the political realm. The counterculture was composed of young people rebelling against the conservatism of the times; with their "hippie" clothing, sit-ins, new music, drug use, and advocacy of "free love" (made less risky in the days before AIDS by the invention of the birth control pill), the movement was experienced by many of their elders as a repudiation of The World As We've Known It. New media—in this case, the underground press—served as a unifying force for many of the young members of the counterculture, much as the Internet today has brought together political activists and reformers.

Entire books have been written about the deeply wrenching events of the Sixties, their consequences, and their meaning, but for purposes of our discussion, it is the institutional failures of trust that are most significant. Preeminent among those, of course, was Watergate. *Watergate* is also often used as shorthand, as a general term meant to encompass a series of political scandals during the administration of President Richard M. Nixon. The triggering event, the burglary that led to the unraveling of the Nixon administration, began when five men were arrested after what first appeared to be commonplace break-in and robbery at the offices of the Democratic National Committee in 1972. (The DNC's offices were in the Watergate complex; hence the scandal's name.) Revelation of the administration's effort to cover up the real nature of the break-in eventually led to Nixon's resignation.

Investigations conducted by the FBI and various congressional committees uncovered a number of other Nixon administration activities that were clearly illegal. They included campaign fraud, political espionage and "dirty tricks" (illegal break-ins to gain strategically useful information, politically motivated tax audits), illegal wiretapping, and a secret pot of money that had been "laundered" in Mexico, from which the administration had paid the people who engaged in these activities. These investigations played out in the media over a period of nearly two years, during which time many activities of the federal government came to a virtual standstill. In the wake of the scandals, the Senate voted to establish an eleven-member investigating body along the lines of the just-concluded Watergate Committee that had conducted the original investigations. The committee was chaired by Senator Frank Church (D-Idaho), from whom it later took its name. Other members included its vice-chairman, John Tower (R-Texas), Walter Mondale (D-Minnesota), and "Mr. Conservative," Barry Goldwater (R-Arizona). Over a period of nine months, the committee interviewed over 800 officials, and held 250 executive and 21 public hearings, probing widespread intelligence abuses by the CIA, FBI, and NSA.[4] When the Church Committee made its report, Congress passed legislation—including the bill familiarly known as FISA, or the Foreign Intelligence Surveillance Act—intended to ensure that future administrations would adhere to the rule of law.

Obviously, the cultural upheavals of the Sixties cannot all be laid at Richard Nixon's feet. But rather than acting as a stabilizing institution, an island of continuity in the sea of change that was the Sixties, the corruption of the Nixon White House deepened national anxiety and exacerbated cynicism and social distrust. At a time when social tensions were already high, the country went through a two-year period where government was simply unable to draw on reservoirs of institutional credibility to ameliorate those tensions. Whatever the failures of subsequent administrations, until recently America has not experienced a similar level of lawlessness on the part of our national government.

IT ALL STARTS IN WASHINGTON

It is easy to point a finger at Washington as the source of much of what ails us. After all, government has been the favorite target of critics and malcontents since Socrates drank that cup of hemlock. What are the grounds for the belief (held by a substantial majority of Americans, if polls are to be believed) that the Bush administration was any worse—any less trustworthy—than those that preceded it, even including the Nixon administration? What are the standards against which we measure the quality of government performance? In other words, what are the characteristics of a trustworthy state, and what are the grounds for the public's perception that the US government under George W. Bush lacked those characteristics?

Those of us who teach public administration and public policy like to use words like "transparency" and "accountability" when we describe the attributes of institutional integrity. What those terms mean in simple English is that citizens should be able to figure out who is in charge of what, and who made what decision and why, so that they can make informed decisions when they next go to the polls. It isn't rocket science, but it does get considerably more complicated as government agencies proliferate and government takes on more and more responsibilities. The sheer size and scope of today's government makes it more difficult to achieve the sort of transparency upon which accountability ultimately depends. It also makes it more important.

There are a number of scholars who focus on these issues,

and whose work identifies reasonable standards by which we can and do evaluate the performance of our governing institutions. There have also been studies of the relationship between effective government and public trust. In 1998, Valerie Braithwaite and Margaret Levi edited one such book: a series of essays exploring and debating the interrelationship between governance practices and public trust.[5] The chapters in the book grew out of conferences held by the Research School of Social Sciences at Australia's National University, and because the contributors synthesized much of the available research, it is worth discussing in some detail.

In one chapter, "Trust in Government," Russell Hardin (perhaps the preeminent scholar working to define and analyze issues of trust) points out that trust in government is a different animal than trust in one's neighbor, spouse, or child; as he notes, most citizens will lack the specific information needed to make a meaningful decision whether to trust government in the sense we trust individuals with whom we interact. That being the case, Hardin sensibly echoes the nation's founders in advocating institutional design that will safeguard citizens against abuses of power and other official malfeasance. Implicit in this recommendation is the notion that "trust" in government is necessarily trust in the integrity and continued effectiveness of that institutional design, rather than in the individuals who may be managing the government enterprise at any particular time.

In another chapter, titled (rather forbiddingly) "Communal and Exchange Trust Norms: Their Value Base and Relevance to Institutional Trust," Valerie Braithwaite argues that trust in government rests on shared social values, as well as the predictability and dependability of government action. In other words, a government that acts on behalf of "us," and that does so in a manner consistent with "our" expectations, is not just instrumental. In an important sense, it is constitutive—that is, by behaving in accordance with our expectations, government becomes an expression of a set of values through which we express our unique national character.

In a particularly acute analysis titled "A State of Trust," Margaret Levi notes the often-overlooked importance of government's contribution to the creation of social capital and generalized trust, and catalogues the institutional arrangements that make governments trustworthy. She finds the most important attributes of a trustworthy state to be "the capacity to monitor laws, bring sanctions against lawbreakers, and provide information and guarantees about those seeking to be trusted. . . . *If citizens doubt the state's commitment to enforce the laws and if its information and guarantees are not credible, then the state's capacity to generate interpersonal trust will diminish*"[6] (emphasis mine). Levi goes on to warn that when citizens don't consider their government trustworthy, the government cannot perform this function. An essential element of its trustworthiness is a belief in the government's *fairness*—what lawyers tend to discuss in terms of due process, equal protection, and the rule of law. A government that plays favorites or that refuses to follow its own rules loses its claim to be trustworthy. (Not incidentally, when citizens lose faith in the credibility of their government, it isn't just trust that suffers: voluntary compliance with the law declines.)

In "Political Trust and the Roots of Devolution," M. Kent Jennings marshals survey data spanning thirty-odd years to demonstrate that Americans' trust in the federal government has steadily declined.[7] He attributes much of that decline to a failure to meet performance expectations, and notes that trust in state and local government units has not ebbed to a similar degree during the period in question. Jennings suggests that this difference in the amount of trust placed in federal and state governments may explain some of the movement toward "devolution" that occurred during the past quarter century. (It is worth noting that the book in which Jennings's chapter appears was published well before the actions of the Bush administration further polarized and alienated Americans.)

In still another thought-provoking analysis, "Trust and Democratic Governance," Tom R. Tyler built on a different series of studies to argue that governments that are widely regarded as procedurally fair, trustworthy, and respectful of their citizens generate social trust by establishing a shared identity.[8] Citizens take pride in their identification with a "good government" and that pride generates both higher levels of compliance with the laws and a belief in the legitimacy of the government.

There are, of course, a multitude of other studies—empirical, theoretical, philosophical, sociological—about the nature and effects of trust in government. Most of them reinforce or elaborate on the points sketched out above. The bottom line is that perceived government legitimacy engenders trust and social capital, and legitimacy is measured by the state's compliance with its own constitutional rules. In America, that sort of legitimacy is particularly important, because fidelity to our constitutional values is what makes the otherwise disparate and diverse residents of this country Americans. It is allegiance to those values that creates whatever *unum* there may be in our *pluribus*.

HAS OUR GOVERNMENT FAILED US? LET US COUNT THE WAYS

As noted above, *Trust and Governance* was published in 1998, two years before the disputed election that brought George W. Bush and his administration to power. Bush's predecessor, Bill Clinton, certainly had not enjoyed universal admiration and support; stories of his womanizing dogged him from early in his first campaign and persisted throughout his two terms in office. Allegations of improper business dealings led to the enormously expensive (and ultimately inconclusive) investigation known as "Whitewater," which in turn led to revelations of sexual improprieties with a White House intern, and an abortive impeachment effort. Widespread use of the nickname "slick Willie" testified to the fact that many Americans did not consider him trustworthy.

For purposes of a discussion of trust in government, however, there is an important difference between Americans' distrust of Clinton and their distrust of George W. Bush and his administration. People who disliked Bill Clinton, who considered him untrustworthy, made that claim based upon his *personal* character. Their disapproval, in fact, was often rooted in a belief that he was not "worthy" of the presidency, that he was "disgracing" the office. The fact that so many of his critics framed the Clinton trust issue in this way is telling, because it conveyed a clear distinction between the (trusted) office of president and its (distrusted) inhabitant. In contrast, complaints about the Bush administration are largely, although certainly not entirely, aimed at its perceived inability to govern competently and especially at the efforts by the president and vice president to evade constitutional restrictions on the power of the executive branch.

Before embarking upon a (necessarily abbreviated and selective) discussion of those complaints, it is important to be very clear about the framework for that discussion. Every administration will pursue policies and make decisions that displease or anger various constituencies. Every officeholder has political and ideological opponents and personal enemies with a vested interest in bringing his or her transgressions and deficiencies to the public's notice. Furthermore, many previous presidents and high-ranking officials have attempted to exercise powers more extensive than those granted by the Constitution, and many have engaged in behaviors—both personal and institutional—that have been less than honorable. (The Nixon administration is the most obvious case in point, but it is far from the only transgressor.) What has distinguished the Bush administration has been its incompetence, the sheer number of ethical and legal transgressions and the magnitude of their consequences, and especially—if belatedly—the widespread public awareness and disapproval of them. It is that heightened awareness that feeds the public's fear that our governing institutions have been hijacked—that our most basic governing structures are no longer reliable. In that sense, whether any particular criticism is fair or unfair is irrelevant; so long as large majorities of Americans believe—as they clearly do—that the very structure of constitutional government has been compromised, that belief alone is enormously consequential for the public trust.

George W. Bush entered office under a cloud: his opponent, Al Gore, had won the popular vote, and the legal wrangling over who would get Florida's electoral vote lasted nearly a month. When the Supreme Court handed Bush the victory, many voters felt disenfranchised, if not robbed.[9] His first few months in office were lackluster, and his approval ratings never rose above the low fifties. Then, of course, the attacks of 9/11 changed the political narrative.

In the wake of 9/11, the president's approval ratings shot into the nineties, as Americans rallied around their commander-in-chief. Over the next six years, however, the president's poll numbers steadily declined, and during his final two years in office, they hovered in the high twenties or low thirties, depending upon the poll. As closely held and tightly run as the administration had been early in its tenure, events that were clearly beyond its control—and its (frequently hamhanded) reactions to those events—were reported on by a media undergoing profound changes. "News management" and "spin control" became steadily less possible—and attempts to exercise such control became more visible. Much of the public's eventual disenchantment was due to old-fashioned incompetence and corruption that—thanks to the aforementioned Internet, twenty-four-hour news networks, and an already polarized electorate—was aggressively publicized. More important, mounting evidence of cronyism and self-dealing made people more willing to distrust the administration's motives in what soon came to be seen as an all-out assault on America's constitutional checks and balances. In the final analysis, the strength and breadth of that assault—easily equal to or greater than that of the Nixon administration[10]—was what distinguished the Bush administration from prior unpopular or inept administrations.

PERFORMANCE CONCERNS

In the aftermath of 9/11, the war in Afghanistan had widespread public support. There was considerably more controversy over Bush's decision to invade Iraq, but a majority of citizens—many of whom believed that Iraq was implicated in the attacks on the World Trade Center[11]—accepted the president's claim that Iraq had weapons of mass destruction and had to be prevented from using them. Few Americans, even those of us opposed to this particular use of American military might, anticipated a lengthy, costly, or bloody struggle; the previous Gulf War had achieved its goal handily. When Bush piloted a Lockheed S-3 Viking aircraft onto the deck of the USS *Abraham Lincoln* aircraft carrier, and strode out in full military regalia to announce that combat operations were over, few Americans (even those of us who found the theatrics excessive) doubted him.

In the aftermath of "victory," however, things didn't look so rosy. Television cameras caught the widespread looting of Iraqi museums and public buildings. Weapons of mass destruc-

tion were nowhere to be found. An insurgency steadily esca-
lated into what looked to most onlookers like a religious civil
war. The new Iraqi government proved incapable of mediating
Sunni-Shiite differences, or even of governing. The evening
news reported mounting American deaths amid growing Iraqi
violence that the troops were unable to prevent.

Little by little, other discomfiting facts became public: the
much-hyped "rescue" of Jessica Lynch that turned out to have
been staged by army "news managers"; the effort to cover up
the fact that football hero Pat Tillman had been killed by
friendly fire; the claim (in Bush's 2003 State of the Union
speech) about yellowcake uranium that proved to be untrue.
The publication of photographs from the prison at Abu
Ghraib, showing young American soldiers taunting and
abusing chained, hooded prisoners, dealt a body-blow to
American self-respect (not to mention our international reputation). It became more and more difficult to excuse each new
revelation as an aberration, a failure of intelligence, an
instance of human error, or the work of "a few bad apples."
Much as the then new medium of television had brought vivid
images of the Vietnam War into America's living rooms in the
Sixties, the proliferation of camera phones and the global availability of the Internet made it difficult, if not impossible, to
avoid unpleasant realities about the conduct of the war.

Less visual, but no less frequent, were reports about questionable government contracting practices, which coinciden-
tally tended to favor companies with long-standing business
and political ties to President Bush and Vice President Cheney.
Story after story described huge, lucrative, no-bid contracts
awarded to companies like Halliburton, where Dick Cheney
had been CEO, and Bechtel, run by former Reagan official
George Schultz. As the war dragged on, disclosures multiplied.
Among the most widely publicized: poor or nonexistent oversight that made it impossible to account for billions of dollars.

Among the most egregious: employees of Blackwater, a private security firm employed by the State Department, were accused of wanton, unprovoked killings of Iraqi civilians; employees of Kellogg Brown and Root, a Halliburton spin-off, were accused of raping a female employee and confining her for several days in a shipping container to keep her from going to the authorities. (These were "made for TV" scandals, and—like the revelations about Jessica Lynch and Pat Tillman—were even more widely covered than the more systemic, but less titillating, stories about constitutional lapses or financial mismanagement.)

Most corrosive of all, as evidence accumulated about the events surrounding the initial decision to go to war, many Americans concluded that the president had intentionally lied to them. These weren't just charges leveled by Democrats or other political opponents. In 2002, Ron Reagan, son of Republican icon Ronald Reagan, wrote a widely circulated article for *Esquire* magazine titled "The Case against George W. Bush," in which he used the *L* word: liar.[12] John Dean, former White House counsel in the Nixon administration, wrote articles (and later, books), accusing the Bush administration of deception.[13] A book by political reporter Ron Susskind was based upon information supplied by Paul O'Neill, Bush's first treasury secretary, and claimed that Bush and Cheney had discussed invading Iraq even before 9/11.[14] The book was widely reviewed and debated, as was an even more critical one written by Richard Clarke, who had served as Bush's counterterrorism chief, a post he had previously held through several administrations, Republican and Democratic.[15] The media also carried reports about a spate of unusually public protests from within the ranks of longtime civil servants. Operatives at the CIA and the Defense Intelligence Agency formed "Veteran Intelligence Professionals for Sanity" and issued a letter accusing the administration of deliberately "warping" intelligence for political purposes. An unusually public letter of resignation from a career diplomat, John Brady Kiesling, raised similar issues, and for a time was one of the most frequently forwarded documents on the Internet.[16] A full accounting of all of the accusations, conspiracy theories, and protests would fill hundreds of pages.

Had the accusations and recriminations been limited to the war in Iraq, they might have done less damage to the nation's trust in its governing institutions. But at the same time acrimony over Iraq was growing, media outlets were filled with evidence of official Washington's corruption. Enron had imploded early in 2001, amid charges that its CEO, Kenneth Lay, had used his friendship with Bush and Cheney to deflect regulatory scrutiny of Enron's business practices. (On June 28, 2002, then Senate majority leader Tom Daschle accused the Republicans of "fostering malfeasance" not just at Enron, but at WorldCom, ImClone, and other companies, giving voice to what were, by then, widespread allegations of official misconduct.)[17] A lawsuit by a public interest organization alleged that Vice President Cheney had allowed a group of handpicked energy company executives to write the administration's energy policy—a lawsuit the vice president fought not on the merits, but by asserting executive privilege. The administration's ties to the energy industry were also blamed for its efforts to downplay the danger posed by global warming, and for what came to be called its "war on science."

Subsequent government scandals were even more widely reported. Tom DeLay, the enormously powerful Republican majority leader of the House of Representatives, was indicted and resigned his seat in Congress. Lobbyist Jack Abramoff—a K Street figure tied to both the White House and Republican members of Congress—eventually cooperated with investigators in return for a shorter prison sentence, implicating several highly placed officials. For weeks the media headlined new revelations about expensive trips and meals Abramoff had provided to various congressmen and members of the administration, and the quid pro quos those favors reportedly purchased. Representative Randy "Duke" Cunningham resigned and went to prison, giving a tearful apology for taking bribes. (That apology was replayed so frequently on television that a few years later the popular political blog, *Talking Points Memo*, inaugurated a mock contest in which it awarded a "Golden Duke" for the most outrageous official misbehavior, confident that readers would have no difficulty recognizing the reference.)

Florida congressman Mark Foley, who had crusaded against pedophiles, resigned after he was found to have sent inappropriate sexual text messages to underage congressional interns, and Idaho senator Larry Craig, a self-styled "family-values" opponent of civil rights for gays and lesbians, was arrested in an airport men's room for soliciting sex. Americans watching the national news at dinnertime got an ever-growing litany of corrupt behavior, political favoritism, and blatant hypocrisy with their burgers and fries.[18]

Some of these transgressions might have been excused, had there been a sense that the administration was discharging the bulk of its governing responsibilities effectively, but evidence to the contrary was everywhere. Politically connected but otherwise unqualified appointees were accused of muzzling government scientists whose conclusions displeased energy interests. FEMA's bungled response to Hurricane Katrina was the lead story on every news broadcast for months, and President Bush's early and unfortunate compliment to then FEMA head Michael Brown—"Heck of a job, Brownie"—is still good for a laugh on late-night talk shows. Despite the president's constant admonition to Americans to "support the troops," investigative reporters repeatedly documented the administration's own deficiencies of support: insufficient supplies of bulletproof vests and Humvee armor, reductions in veterans' benefits, and most vividly, the seriously substandard conditions at Walter Reed

Hospital, where many of the troops wounded in Iraq and Afghanistan were being treated. For several days, television cameras panned relentlessly over bandaged soldiers, moldy walls, and cockroach-infested hospital rooms. Meanwhile, as the war dragged on, a chorus of retired generals critical of its conduct was endlessly recycled by news channels and talk shows.

THE CONSTITUTIONAL ASSAULTS

Just forty-five days after 9/11, Congress passed the USA Patriot Act, granting greatly expanded powers to the federal government. Some of the provisions had been on the Justice Department's "wish list" for years, but had met resistance in Congress; others were intended to assist the newly declared War on Terror. The Patriot Act expanded terrorism laws to include "domestic terrorism," a provision that critics charged could be used to justify surveillance of disfavored political organizations, and authorized secret searches, dubbed "sneak and peek." It allowed investigations of American citizens without probable cause if the FBI asserted the investigation was "related" to terrorism. Section 215 was perhaps the most criticized of all sections of the act: among other things, it required librarians to provide the FBI with lists of books checked out or Web sites visited by a person the bureau was investigating; worse, the search could be accompanied by a "gag" order preventing the librarian from disclosing the fact of the investigation to anyone. As the terms of the Patriot Act became known to the broader public, it engendered enormous—and generally bipartisan[19]—criticism; a large number of city councils and several state legislatures passed resolutions condemning it.

As the Iraq War continued, and antiwar sentiment grew, administration officials took steps to curb dissent—or as many saw it, suppress the exercise of protesters' First Amendment rights. The Secret Service established "Free Speech Zones" to keep dissenters away from the president and vice president when they traveled. People who disagreed with Bush's policies were accused by administration officials (most notably, then attorney general John Ashcroft and Vice President Cheney) of aiding terrorists.

Reports surfaced about efforts the administration had made to punish even obscure citizens who cast doubt on administration veracity. In New Mexico, a nurse with the Veterans Administration was told she was being investigated for sedition and might lose her job because she wrote a letter to the editor criticizing George W. Bush and advocating withdrawal from Iraq. This, despite the fact that the letter was signed in her private capacity as a citizen, written on her own time, and on her own stationery. In Washington, DC, Lewis Fisher, a thirty-six-year veteran of the Congressional Research Agency and widely considered the most eminent living scholar of the doctrine of separation of powers, was told to "apologize" and threatened with loss of his position in the wake of a research report disputing presidential authority to ignore Congress and engage in unchecked surveillance of Americans' communications. He had served with distinction under Republican and Democratic administrations alike. While not as publicly covered as the misnamed "Free Speech Zones," news of these and similar episodes circulated widely within relevant constituencies.

By far the most widely publicized incident of retaliation involved former ambassador Joseph Wilson. Wilson wrote a much-discussed op-ed for the *New York Times* in which he disputed the president's claim that Saddam Hussein had sought to purchase yellowcake uranium from the African nation of Niger. In response, the administration leaked the fact that Wilson's wife, Valerie Plame, was a covert CIA agent. The revelation destroyed her career, and may have endangered the lives of other covert agents. A lengthy—and extensively covered—investigation by Deputy Attorney General Patrick Fitzgerald ran into a brick wall in the person of Lewis "Scooter" Libby, the vice president's chief of staff. Fitzgerald ultimately charged Libby with lying to the grand jury, and brought him to trial. After Libby was convicted of perjury, President Bush immediately commuted his sentence. The message was clear: people who challenge the administration do so at their peril; those who are loyal to the administration will be protected.

Throughout its tenure, the Bush administration aggressively advanced a view of executive power that has been roundly rejected by most legal scholars. This theory, dubbed the "Unitary Executive," places the presidency on a more-than-equal footing with the legislative and judicial branches of government, and endorses a presidential power that is not just muscular, but, as the libertarian Cato Institute has argued,

astonishingly broad, a view that includes

- A federal government empowered to regulate core political speech—and restrict it greatly when it counts the most: in the days before a federal election;
- A president who cannot be restrained, through validly enacted statutes, from pursuing any tactic he believes to be effective in the war on terror;
- A president who has the inherent constitutional authority to designate American citizens suspected of terrorist activity as 'enemy combatants' and lock them up without charges for the duration of the war on terror—in other words, perhaps forever; and
- A federal government with the power to supervise virtually every aspect of American life, from kindergarten, to marriage, to the grave.[20]

Some of the administration's persistent efforts to avoid accountability were comic: for example, an executive order requires that all members of the executive branch who are entitled to see classified documents cooperate with the National Archives to ensure that sensitive materials are protected. For four years, Vice President Cheney refused to comply, claiming that the law (like so many others) didn't apply to him because the vice president is not part of the executive branch. As several commentators noted, this position raised some fascinating questions, among them why, if Cheney wasn't a member of the executive branch, he so often claimed executive privilege, and why his office's expenses (and his salary) were part of the executive branch budget.

Other administration positions were less amusing. For example, as we all learn in high school government class, the Constitution specifies the manner in which a bill becomes law: Congress drafts and passes legislation, which it sends to the president. If the president vetoes the measure, it fails, unless Congress responds with enough votes to override the veto. If the president signs the legislation, he issues a press release, hands out commemorative pens, and the bill becomes law.

The Bush administration found a way to avoid that constitutional process, by treating what are called "signing statements" as functional line-item vetoes.[21] When Congress passed a bill with provisions Bush didn't like, he went ahead and signed it. But along with the usual (publicly distributed) press release, he quietly issued his own "constitutional interpretation" of the legislation. If these signing statements had simply reflected his concern about the new law's consistency with the Constitution, that would be fair enough; the president takes an oath to uphold the Constitution, and if he believes otherwise necessary legislation contains provisions that are unconstitutional, he is certainly entitled to say so. In the past, lacking a line-item veto, presidents have used signing statements when a questionable measure has been attached to an otherwise important bill. In the Reagan administration, such statements were used as a not-so-subtle signal to federal agencies about how the president (their boss) wanted the law to be interpreted and applied. Bush went further; he used signing statements to signal his intention to simply *ignore* provisions with which he disagreed. This turned the statements into the equivalents of vetoes—with one very important added political benefit: the tactic not only deprived Congress of its constitutional right to override, but for a considerable period of time, it kept most reporters and voters from noticing.

By the time the *Boston Globe* called attention to the practice in 2006, Bush had "quietly claimed the authority to disobey more than 750 laws enacted since he took office, asserting that he has the power to set aside any statute passed by Congress when it conflicts with his interpretation of the Constitution."[22]

The media and public had remained largely unaware of this strategy until passage of the very high-profile McCain Amendment. Sponsored by Republican Senator (and later, 2008 Republican nominee for president) John McCain, who had himself been tortured as a prisoner during the Vietnam War, the bill outlawed torture of detainees. It was strenuously opposed by the administration. When Bush signed it, a signing statement expressed his intent to "construe" the act in a manner consistent with his preferred interpretations of both presidential authority to "protect the American people" and "limits on judicial power." At that point, signing statements—and the threat they pose to constitutional checks and balances—became the subject of widespread publicity and discussion.

Even higher profile was the ongoing debate over domestic spying. The administration secretly authorized the NSA to "mine" enormous amounts of data obtained by "monitoring" (i.e., listening and reading) vast numbers of telephone calls and e-mails—without, however, going to the trouble of obtaining a warrant. The courts were given no role in reviewing this assertion of executive authority; instead, an NSA shift supervisor was allowed to sign off on the warrantless surveillance of Americans. As numerous lawyers pointed out, that's neither a check nor a balance. As they also pointed out, if speed and secrecy were concerns, government officials needing authorization for domestic spying could have gone to the special Foreign Intelligence Surveillance Act (FISA) Court set up by Congress in 1978 for that purpose. The FISA Court can approve eavesdropping in hours, even minutes, if necessary; furthermore, the law specifically allows the government to eavesdrop on its own in a pinch, and justify its action to the court retroactively. (Nor could the FISA Court be accused of being obstructionist; between 1979 and 2005, out of tens of thousands of requests, it had denied exactly four.) Congress's purpose in establishing this semisecret court was to ensure that federal power would not be misused, that it would not be deployed against political enemies or dissenters who simply disagreed with government policies, as had happened during the Nixon administration. (Think not just of Nixon himself, but also of J. Edgar Hoover's surveillance of "domestic enemies" like Martin Luther King Jr.)

Whatever the constitutional infirmities of this program—and they are considerable—it is unlikely that most Americans could identify them. What they did identify, however, was yet another threat to their rapidly eroding privacy. Major businesses—Amazon, Google, doctors, insurance companies—were amassing huge amounts of data on virtually every American. Identity theft had become a growing concern. And now, the media was filled with allegations that the major telephone companies had willingly sold customer records to the government and engaged in illegal spying on those same customers at the government's behest.

The background to each of these conflicts was the implicit

challenge to a constitutional system built on checks and balances. The nation's founders had very good reasons for establishing a system that did not require citizens to simply trust that unlimited power would be exercised responsibly, and most of us consider those reasons—if anything—more compelling today. The issue is not whether a majority of American citizens agree with any particular decision made, or action taken, by a particular administration; the issue is whether the decision or action was legitimate, that is, whether the applicable rules were followed. If the president is above the law, if—as Bush asserted under his theory of the "Unitary Executive"—he has "inherent power" to do anything he and he alone decides is "necessary," there *is* no law. Most Americans who were following the arguments over government surveillance and the FISA Court recognized that the administration's claims to such power were contrary to the rule of law as we had historically understood it.

Even Americans who were not following the news closely, however, were aware of the allegations of lawlessness, concerns that were raised again when eight US Attorneys—all appointees of President George W. Bush and all well-regarded by their peers—were abruptly dismissed. When challenged about the highly unusual terminations, the administration pointed out that those who had been discharged served "at the pleasure of the president," and could be fired for no reason at all, which was true. "No reason," however, is not the same as an improper reason. As Bud Cummins, one of the eight fired prosecutors, explained in an article written for *Salon*, the online magazine, a dismissal should never be based upon the prosecutor's unwillingness to break the rules to "help" favored politicians:

> Put simply, the Department of Justice lives on credibility.
> When a federal prosecutor sends FBI agents to your

brother's house with an arrest warrant, demonstrating an intention to take away years of his liberty, separate him from his family, and take away his property, you and the public at large must have absolute confidence that the sole reason for those actions is that there was substantial evidence to suggest that your brother intentionally committed a federal crime. Everyone must have confidence that the prosecutor exercised his or her vast discretion in a neutral and nonpartisan pursuit of the facts and the law.[23]

We might draw an instructive analogy to judicial selection. Everyone understands that the party in power can appoint federal judges whose judicial philosophy it favors. Would we then shrug our shoulders and say "politics as usual" if judicial appointments went to people who had promised in advance to rule on cases the way the administration wanted? Of course not. Choosing someone with a compatible judicial philosophy is one thing; choosing someone who is corrupt is another. Most Americans appeared to understand the difference, especially as other administration lawyers came forward with stories of their own.

One of those who came forward was Joseph D. Rich. Rich had served in the Justice Department for thirty-five years, and was chief of the voting rights section from 1999 to 2005. As he wrote in the *Los Angeles Times*, he worked under attorneys general with very different political philosophies, from "John Mitchell to Ed Meese to Janet Reno. Regardless of the administration, the political appointees had respect for the experience and judgment of longtime civil servants." Not so the Bush administration, he charged, which hired and fired solely on the basis of political loyalty:

I personally was ordered to change performance evaluations of several attorneys under my supervision. I was told to include critical comments about those whose recommendations ran counter to the political will of the administration and to improve evaluations of those who were politically favored.[24]

Extensive media coverage of these and other charges and countercharges, and testimony at the congressional investigation called to probe the reasons for the firings, appeared to confirm the charge that the eight US Attorneys had been dismissed because they refused to play politics—refused to bring bogus charges against Democrats, or to suppress investigations of high-ranking Republicans. Needless to say, such allegations are enormously corrosive of trust in the American justice system.

Add to these examples the ongoing, passionate, and very public debates being waged over numerous other assertions of administration power at the expense of the Constitution and long-standing legal traditions: holding people at Guantanamo for years without charging them with any crime; denying detainees the right of habeas corpus; rendition,[25] the use of "enhanced" interrogation techniques we used to call torture; and too many others to list. As persistent, serious allegations filled broadcasts, newsmagazines, newspapers, and blogs, and as the "viral" nature of the Internet[26] delivered those allegations to huge audiences that would have been unlikely to see them in the past, is it any wonder that the American people became ever more distrustful of their governing institutions? Or that less-powerful and less-privileged Americans, and those from historically marginalized groups, displayed lower levels of trust than did those Americans who were in a position to "work" the system?

TRUST, FEAR, AND POWERLESSNESS

Most Americans do not follow political news carefully. The process through which average citizens form their opinions about the state of their governing institutions is complex, and the so-called conventional wisdom of any time is the product of many kinds and sources of information. Public consensus is notoriously slow to arrive (and even slower to be displaced). It wasn't until the Bush administration was in its second term that a majority of Americans (at least, judging from available polls) believed it to be untrustworthy. Unfortunately, they had no trusted alternative to which they could turn. If Bush's approval numbers were abysmal—and they were—Congress fared little better. Americans had returned the Democrats to control in 2006, but for a variety of reasons, some understandable, many not, Congress did little during the following year to confront the administration, to insist upon adherence to the Constitution, or to make the major policy changes (most notably, setting a time for withdrawal from Iraq) that a majority of Americans thought they had voted for. The perception that the beneficiaries of the 2006 vote had failed to effect real change added to the frustration and feelings of powerlessness that were feeding the public mood.

Many commentators have remarked upon the fearfulness that characterized much of the electorate in the wake of 9/11 and for several years thereafter. Those events had certainly bewildered and frightened many people, but the fears that have lingered are not just fears of terrorism (a fear that has been cynically exploited by politicians of both parties, although mostly by the GOP). Other, equally destabilizing fears and uncertainties are rooted in systemic problems and challenges that long preceded the Bush administration.

As increasing numbers of Americans lost health insurance,

they worried about medical catastrophes; as outsourcing sent even white-collar jobs overseas, they worried about their own and their families' future security. Major employers downsized as they lost their competitive edge and market share. As gas prices rose steadily, a country more dependent than most on the personal automobile and the availability of cheap energy felt the squeeze. As general economic conditions worsened, people who had not previously experienced financial insecurity found themselves in increasingly tenuous situations. Mortgage foreclosures moved from low-income neighborhoods into pricier precincts, and the boarded-up windows became a grim reminder that middle-class Americans are not always exempt from hard times.

If the business cycle and periodic economic downturns have long been a fact of economic life, the threat posed by global warming has not. After decades during which Congress and much of the business community dismissed global warming as a fiction of the "tree huggers," a series of natural disasters linked to climate change brought home the reality and severity of the threat.

All of these problems—terrorism, the environment, the global economy, the healthcare system, the energy crisis—have at least one thing in common: individuals can't fix them. They require collective efforts, and our ability to take effective collective action depends upon the vitality and trustworthiness of our common institutions—primarily, government. But everything Americans have heard, read, and been told for the better part of the last decade has added up to one message: our government is broken. Worse, for a long time we have seemed powerless to fix it.

The election of 2000 had highlighted the drawbacks of the Electoral College. Devised at a time when America had fewer than 3 million people widely dispersed among the colonies, the Electoral College has become increasingly irrelevant to the

2000 (2001); Doug Keller, *Grand Theft 2000: Media Spectacle and a Stolen Election* (2001).

10. See, for example, John Dean's book, *Worse Than Watergate*. Dean was a member of the Nixon administration who saw firsthand the scope of its illegal activities.

11. A belief the administration artfully cultivated without ever explicitly asserting it.

12. Ron Reagan, "The Case against George W. Bush," *Esquire*, September 1, 2004.

13. John Dean, "Missing Weapons of Mass Destruction: Is Lying about the Reasons for War an Impeachable Offense?" *Findlaw's Legal Commentary*, June 6, 2003.

14. Ron Susskind, *The Price of Loyalty: George W. Bush, the White House, and the Education of Paul O'Neill* (New York: Simon & Schuster, 2004).

15. Richard Clarke, *Against All Enemies: Inside America's War on Terror* (New York: Free Press, 2004).

16. John Brady Kiesling, "U.S. Diplomat's Letter of Resignation," *New York Times*, February 27, 2003.

17. William Saletan, *Bearing Right: How Conservatives Won the Abortion War* (Berkeley: University of California Press, 2004).

18. Scandals involving money and sex have always been around. Journalists will argue that one reason for protecting a free press is so that citizens will have an independent institution monitoring government behavior. But trust in the media is, if anything, lower than trust in government, and it was not helped by revelations that the GOP and the administration had paid newspaper columnists for favorable coverage, despite antipropaganda laws that would seem to forbid such practices.

19. One of the strongest critics was former Georgia representative Bob Barr, a very conservative Republican, who worked with the ACLU to try to overturn the more egregious provisions of the Patriot Act. Barr later left the GOP and ran for president in 2008 on the Libertarian ticket.

20. Gene Healy and Timothy Lynch, *Power Surge: The Constitutional Record of George W. Bush* (Washington, DC: Cato Institute, 2006), p. 1.

21. The Supreme Court has held that a line-item veto is unconstitutional, because it violates the separation of powers.

22. Charlie Savage, "Bush Challenges Hundreds of Laws: President Cites Powers of His Office," *Boston Globe*, April 30, 2006.

23. Bud Cummins, "How Bush's Justice Department Has 'Blown It,'" *Salon*, March 31, 2007, http://www.salon.com/opinion/feature/2007/03/31/cummins/ (accessed August 26, 2008).

24. Joseph D. Rich, "Bush's Long History of Tilting Justice," *Los Angeles Times*, March 29, 2007.

25. *Rendition* was the name given to a secret practice of sending prisoners to prisons in other countries for interrogation. These "black sites" were in nations where torture was commonplace.

26. It is difficult to overestimate the extent to which the Internet has changed the political and information landscape. Cyberspace remains in its infancy when it comes to *generating* news through original reporting, but it is far and away the most efficient news *distribution* mechanism we have ever seen.

27. Typically, redistricting occurs every ten years, following the completion of the national census. The effort to force an extra redistricting was thus transparently political.

Chapter 6

THE TRUST GAP

Who Trusts, Who "Turtles," and Why?

It would be great if we could explain declining social trust entirely as a logical response to our disquieting external realities, but of course, in the social sciences nothing is quite that simple. Putnam concluded that people who live in more diverse neighborhoods are less trusting than those who live in more homogeneous communities. That means that their levels of generalized trust are even lower than the low levels that currently characterize Americans generally. And apparently, it doesn't matter whether the residents of those diverse neighborhoods are members of the majority or the minority—they are *all* less trusting. Other research, on balance, supports that conclusion. So the questions that prompted this inquiry remain: Why do diverse neighborhoods produce lower levels of generalized trust than the levels that characterize society as a whole? Is it living with difference that makes us more wary?

Or are the lower trust levels connected in some fashion to the nature of the places that we live—places that are also likely to be diverse? (Hint: that would be cities.)

REVISITING THE QUESTION

Common sense may suggest that the past decade has given Americans ample reason to approach our collective life with skepticism, but those reasons have still left us without an explanation for the differences between diverse neighborhoods and others. In fact, we are left with a number of unanswered questions, all of which bear on the relationship between diversity and distrust: Why are people who live in cities more distrustful than those who live in smaller, more rural environments? Why do those who inhabit more diverse neighborhoods trust less and "turtle" more than those from more homogeneous communities? Why do women and African Americans trust less?

If national events and institutional failures were the sole explanation for low levels of trust, wouldn't the decline be more uniform? And how do we explain the very counterintuitive tendency for inhabitants of our most diverse cities—the very inhabitants who have been identified as *least* trusting and *most* turtled—to be far more likely to support liberal candidates and expanded social welfare policies (policies that will clearly benefit the presumably distrusted "others") than are residents of rural and suburban areas? If they are really less engaged in their communities, less trusting of their neighbors, why are so many of them willing to pay higher taxes to improve those communities and assist those neighbors? Can we make sense of any of this?

We can't explain why diversity might deepen distrust without considering the reasons people develop trust in the first place. If we can identify the elements most likely to engender trust, we can then examine diverse neighborhoods and discrete populations to see which of those elements may be missing. Unfortunately, even a cursory look at the research on social trust uncovers multiple areas of debate and uncertainty. Scholars disagree about the nature of social trust and its role in creating and sustaining social capital. They disagree on definitions of social capital. They disagree about how to measure either one. They debate varying theories about the relationship of trust and social capital to the performance of government and social institutions. And they propose multiple theories about where trust comes from in the first place. (There is even recent medical research that links trust in humans to levels of oxytocin, a neuropeptide that has been shown to play a key role in social attachment and affiliation in other mammals.)[1]

Despite the conflicting scholarship, however, we can find useful clues. In 1992, Jan Delhey and Kenneth Newton wrote a particularly helpful article in which they reviewed most of the research that had previously been done on social trust, and asked a pertinent question: "What sorts of people express social trust and distrust, and under what sorts of social, economic and political circumstances do they do so?"[2] In other words, who trusts and why? They mined the (extensive) available literature and identified six main theories of social trust, which they divided into two individual and four social theories, and which they then tested against survey data from seven nations. The individual theories were 1) *Personality*, a theory resting on social-psychological factors (that is, this theory describes social trust as part of a particular personality type—as an attribute of people who are optimistic, who believe in cooperation, and who believe that reasonable people can sit down and resolve their differences); and 2) *Success and Well-Being* (this is the theory that social trust is associated with society's "winners," and that distrust is more common among the "losers"—those with poor educations, lower incomes and status, and those who are generally dissatisfied with their lives). Personality theory tends to emphasize the importance of childhood socialization, while the success and well-being theory stresses adult life experience. In both categories, however, trust is identified as an individual characteristic.

In contrast to the two individual theories, societal theories begin with the assumption that generalized trust is a social property—an attribute of the culture within which the individual functions. Those who approach social trust from this perspective believe expressions of trust are based upon the individual's estimation of the trustworthiness of the larger society. Delhey and Newton identified four types of societal theory: 1) the *Voluntary Associations Theory* (with which Putnam is identified, and which posits that we learn trust from participation in voluntary and communal organizations); 2) *Network Theory* (which sees trust as an outgrowth of participation in the informal networks of daily life—family, friends, co-workers, and the like); 3) *Community Theory* (the belief that trust correlates with the demographic characteristics of the communities within which individuals reside—size, population density, etc.); and 4) *Societal Theory* (people who live in wealthier nations with democratic governments, greater income equality, more universal social welfare systems, independent courts, and political controls over the power of politicians are more trusting than those who live in societies that lack these characteristics). Community theory is sometimes referred to as a "bottom up" explanation, while societal theory is "top down," or institutional.

Delhey and Newton prefaced their description of survey research results with a reminder that *correlation* is not the same thing as *causation*, and that even in situations where an association is identified, causation often remains difficult to determine. As they caution,

The study of trust is benighted by the problem of cause and effect. Do people become more trusting as a result of close and sustained interaction with others in voluntary organizations? Or is it, on the contrary, that trusting people join voluntary associations and get involved with their community, leaving distrusting ones at home to watch the television? Do people develop higher levels of trust because life has been kind to them, or is life kind to them because they are trusting?[3]

When Delhey and Newton tested the six theories they had identified against survey data from seven countries— Germany, Hungary, Slovenia, South Korea, Spain, and Switzerland—they found little support for the social-psychological theory that attributed social trust to early socialization or personality type. Putnam notwithstanding, they also found little or no association between levels of trust and membership in voluntary organizations, or between trust and city size, type of community, or neighborhood satisfaction. Trust was also unrelated to age, gender, or even education (except to the extent that better education was a factor in success and well-being, factors which *were* related to trust).

Other theories, however, did prove to have explanatory power. First, social conditions—particularly the presence or absence of social conflict and public safety—were robust predictors of trust: where there was social conflict and/or the absence of public safety and personal security, there was less social trust. As the authors pointed out, this finding is consistent with the theory that socially homogeneous societies— with shared social norms and low levels of social conflict—are likely to have higher levels of trust than societies with "deep social and economic cleavages."[4] It is also consistent with research that has identified fear as one of the most powerful— and generally detrimental—social motivators.

Second, although membership in voluntary associations was unrelated to levels of social trust, membership in informal social networks *was* positively related to trust. (This should be good news, since some research suggests that participation in these informal networks—in distinction to more formal associations—is growing.)

Third, the success and well-being theory performed well. As the authors noted, "There is, it seems, quite a lot in the suggestion that those who are successful in life can afford to trust more."[5] They found that anxiety scores—highest among low-income and low-status groups and the unemployed—were predictive of higher levels of distrust. And interestingly, the two countries that registered lowest in levels of social trust in this study were the two that had most recently experienced significant political and social changes. Despite their reticence about assigning cause and effect, Delhey and Newton concluded that "lack of trust is not the cause of social and political upheaval and conflict in these countries, but the expression of them."[6]

The Delhey and Newton results are consistent with points raised by several social capital researchers. Carles Boix and Daniel Posner have argued that "a community's co-operative capacity is a function of the degree of social and political inequality that the community has experienced over the course of its historical development."[7] The results also lend support to the work of American scholars who criticize social capital theory for its failure to adequately acknowledge the impact of racism and the importance of social justice issues,[8] particularly the wide and growing differences between America's haves and have-nots. There is a significant overlap between the two categories; poor people in America have historically been disproportionately African American or—more recently—members of other minority racial groups.

Interestingly, Putnam's most recent findings have been discussed almost entirely in the context of immigration, rather than race, and his work has been cited—to his obvious dismay—by those who argue that immigration (legal or illegal) is threatening American bonds of social solidarity. This is curious, since Putnam attributed the turtle phenomenon to the extent of ethnic diversity, not to the identity of the people creating it. In much of the United States, "diversity" is most often used as a code word for differences in race, rather than national origin.

Conflicts in the past have certainly centered around differences in cultural ethnicity or religion or immigration, but the central fault line in America has been and continues to be race. It is not coincidental that in our current highly charged and politicized arguments over immigration, the complaints focus first and foremost on immigrants from Latin America, and to a lesser extent, those from Asia. (My son-in-law, a Caucasian who immigrated from England twenty-eight years ago, has yet to experience discrimination—or even hear a disapproving remark—based upon his immigration status. And no one, to my knowledge, has suggested building a fence between the United States and Canada.) It is hard to know the degree to which current anti-immigrant sentiment is masking racial hostility, the direct expression of which—thankfully—is no longer countenanced in respectable society. Both America's racial history and our tolerance for economic inequality sets us apart from other Western democracies, and it should come as no surprise that comparative research confirms this unfortunate aspect of American "exceptionalism."[9]

THE DIVERSITY EFFECT

If Delhey and Newton are correct in their reading of the available research, the factors that reduce trust are the presence of social conflict, concerns about public safety, reduced partici-

pation in informal networks, and anxiety, especially economic anxiety. All of these factors tend to be present in
America's urban centers, where—despite the growing diversity of the nation's suburbs—the bulk of our diverse neighborhoods can still be found. As a recent study by the Urban
Center concluded:

> More than half of all neighborhoods in America's 100 largest
> metropolitan areas (56.6 percent) are home to significant
> numbers of whites, minorities and immigrants, with no
> single racial or ethnic group dominating the minority popu-
> lation. Six of ten (60.8 percent) are mixed-income—domi-
> nated neither by households in the highest income quintiles
> nor by those in the lowest. And about a third of all tracts
> (34.9 percent) exhibit substantial diversity with respect to
> age, ethnicity and income.[10]

If we look both at the factors that generate distrust and the
characteristics of neighborhoods where the greatest diversity is
to be found, it isn't difficult to confirm the overlap:

- In central city neighborhoods characterized by diversity,
  social conflict is common. Conflicts may take the form of
  interest groups fighting over inadequate municipal
  resources, they may occur as different groups jockey for
  power, or they may arise from miscommunication or
  lack of communication caused by differences in language, lifestyle, or culture. In some of the poorest such
  neighborhoods, in addition to genuine disagreements
  about goals or efforts to access resources, there are often
  the sorts of "street fight" encounters that may be triggered by anything from rival gangs, real or perceived
  slights, or just by the multiple tensions that accompany
  poverty.

- Metropolitan areas struggle to provide public safety. Larger cities also must deal with pervasive negative perceptions about public safety and urban life; even in relatively safe areas and during periods of diminished criminal activity, so-called conventional wisdom reinforces the image of "mean streets," lurking danger, and threatening criminal behaviors. From petty thefts (purse snatching, pickpocketing) to carjackings, burglaries, and violent crimes like murder and rape, crime is a constant concern in many inner-city areas. (It doesn't help that most metropolitan newspapers follow the "if it bleeds, it leads" school of journalism, and accordingly publicize the more gory crimes with banner headlines and front-page, "above the fold" placements. Local broadcast news follows a similar pattern.) Criminologists and those who map the incidence of crime—particularly violent crimes like homicides—will confirm that such crimes are more common in areas having greater population density and even more so in areas having both greater density and substantial poverty. When people do not feel safe, they rarely feel trusting and neighborly.
- In neighborhoods plagued by perceptions of crime and populated by people who look different, follow different customs, eat different foods, and increasingly speak different languages, easy opportunities to engage in the sorts of informal social networking that encourages trusting attitudes are sharply limited.
- Finally, the anxiety that is a predictor of distrust is a constant companion of people living in many central city venues. The United States has one of the least effective and least extensive social welfare systems in the West, and we actively stigmatize dependence on public assistance. We do not have national healthcare, or universal access to healthcare; currently, over 46 million Ameri-

cans are without any health insurance coverage. Add to the insecurity and anxiety that accompany this lack of a social safety net the steady loss of manufacturing and other jobs as industries downsize and outsource in order to remain competitive. Then herd large numbers of these vulnerable citizens (and even more vulnerable noncitizens) into crowded inner-city neighborhoods. It shouldn't be surprising that terms like "success and well-being" are not the first words that come to mind to describe such precincts, nor should it come as a surprise that the resulting levels of stress and anxiety are high. These are frequently people who are without resources or power—and not just political and economic power, but even the power to substantially improve their own lives. Anxiety is a child of powerlessness.

Dealing with unfamiliarity that challenges our worldviews can be stressful under any circumstances, but when ever-increasing pluralism complicates the lives of those who have the fewest personal and fiscal resources for dealing with such challenges, we shouldn't be surprised when the response is withdrawal. Turtles retreat into their shells when they're threatened, and in many of America's inner cities, people live under more or less constant threat.

There are, of course, many people who live in cities—and in diverse neighborhoods—who are not without resources, just as there are many who are civically engaged. Widespread gentrification has brought people of means back to our central cities in large numbers. It would be a mistake, however, to assume that these more fortunate residents can entirely escape the consequences of municipal failures to secure public safety and provide city services. Urban areas are where institutional failures are most apparent, and cities are places where all people, rich and poor, are most dependent upon reliable and

trustworthy public services—not just police and fire depart-
ments, but public transportation, public schools, public parks,
and public works. When urban public institutions fail,
everyone who lives in and around the city feels the effects.

Does diversity add to the stress of urban living? Undoubtedly, for the reasons I elaborated on in chapters 1 and 2. But it
is difficult (and arguably misleading) to pin all the blame for
lower levels of trust on diversity alone, especially when we
can't rule out potential contributions by other elements of
those same environments.

HAVEN'T WE BEEN HERE BEFORE?

American diversity is not a new phenomenon. Optimists
viewing the current state of affairs like to point out that the
history of the United States is a history of making strangers
into (more-or-less) members of the family. Pessimists remind
us that the process has been uneven, often unpleasant, and
constantly contested. Historians have argued strenuously over
the proper metaphor: Is America a melting pot, where cultural
differences are "cooked out," or is it a stew, with different
ingredients providing their unique flavors to the same dish?
Perhaps we should think of the country as a symphony, where
one group plays horns and another strings—different instruments harmonizing to create a single musical composition that
is more than the sum of its parts.

Uplifting as the symphony metaphor may be, however, the
pessimists are right to remind us that American history has
rarely been harmonious. Particularity and identity have stub-
bornly resisted being amalgamated into a more featureless,
more White Anglo-Saxon Protestant, more uniform citizenry.
Furthermore, as a result of slavery, voluntary immigration, and
internal migration, the face and character of the American

majority has undergone constant change, as successive groups of newcomers have been first resisted and then grudgingly accommodated. The process has been anything but smooth, and Emma Lazarus to the contrary, Americans haven't always lifted lamps "beside the Golden Door."[11] Globalization, technology, and terrorism may be raising the stakes, but the tensions caused by diversity and immigration are nothing new.

In fact, American history is a story of repeated encounters with new arrivals, and our less-than-welcoming responses to those newcomers. The Alien and Sedition Acts of 1798 were passed in reaction to fears about the "European radicals" who were coming to the United States (or so it was thought) to destabilize our still-new country. The acts gave the president power to exclude or deport any foreigners he considered dangerous. The acts also gave him the (patently unconstitutional) power to prosecute anyone who criticized the government. At about the same time, in a move that could hardly be considered welcoming, Congress extended the waiting period for immigrants applying to become citizens to fourteen years.

By the 1840s, immigration was bringing large numbers of Irish and German Roman Catholics to American shores. Economic insecurity added fuel to the fire of the resulting Protestant backlash; Evangelical Protestants, especially, decried "papacy" and accused Catholics of bringing crime and disease to America. Protestant workers burned down an Ursuline convent near Boston, and there were anti-Catholic riots in several cities. The unrest led to the formation of the American Party, which was popularly called the "Know-Nothing Party." The Know-Nothings were no small splinter group; they won six governorships and controlled several state legislatures. Ironically, the Know-Nothing Party became a casualty of a different clash over "otherness." The fight over slavery that led to the Civil War divided members of the Know-Nothing Party as it divided friends, families, and states.

The Civil War decided the issue of slavery, but failed to resolve the deeper issues of racism. The nation would go through Jim Crow, segregation, and the civil rights movement before most of the legal impediments to equality were removed. The harder work of erasing systemic discrimination and changing people's hearts and minds is ongoing, and progress—while notable—has come in uneven fits and starts.

While East Coast Nativists focused their hostility on Irish and German immigrants, those on the West Coast targeted the Chinese. The Workingman's Party led a movement to ban the employment of Chinese immigrants, to require them to live apart in "Chinatowns," and even to keep them from entering California. Under pressure from California and other western states, the US Congress passed the Chinese Exclusion Act of 1882.

In the wake of the Civil War, the gap between rich and poor grew wider, pitting working people (including many immigrants) against industrialists who exercised essentially unregulated power. Violent strikes were met with accusations of "European Socialism." Anti-Catholic fervor was high, and secret societies—notably the "American Protective Association"—were able to get laws passed banning instruction in German. (At the time, many Catholic parochial schools taught classes in German.) But by the 1890s, the focus had once again changed. More immigrants were coming from Italy, Greece, Poland, Hungary, and Russia, and fewer from Ireland, England, and Germany. A federal commission was duly charged with studying problems associated with the foreign-born; the commission issued a forty-two-volume "report," alleging (among other things) that the newer immigrants were less skilled, less educated, more "clannish," less likely to learn English, and generally even more undesirable than the older immigrants. The subsequent "Americanization" campaign—conducted by the federal government's Bureau of Americanization—wanted employers to require that their workers learn

English, and many states banned foreign-language education (a legacy of linguistic illiteracy we are still trying to overcome).

Subsequent eruptions of Nativism included the Palmer Raids in the 1920s (during which the FBI deported alien "subversives" without affording those accused of subversive activities any due process), and the introduction of immigration quotas based upon national origin, in order to favor people coming from "genetically superior" countries of origin. Those quotas remained in place until 1965, when they were finally ended by the Immigration Reform Act. Once the quotas were lifted, immigrants flooded in from all over the world, and the resulting increase in diversity led to the English Only movement of the 1980s. In the 1990s, California passed Proposition 187, requiring public agencies to determine the immigration status of people they served and to deny services and arrest those who were undocumented.

These unremitting efforts to disenfranchise, harass, or otherwise retaliate against those who were different were often struck down by the courts. The most punitive laws were eventually repealed. Nativist groups that had organized to disadvantage particular groups died out, and others formed to attack newer threats. Had social scientists equipped with survey instruments been handy during each wave of immigration and antagonism, they would likely have documented diminished trust levels in those diverse neighborhoods as well.

AMERICA'S SECRET WEAPON

As ugly as these and many other episodes have been, Americans new and old have been able to deploy a powerful weapon against bigotry: our particular vision of the just society and its institutions.

Perhaps the most important element of that vision was the

urban archipelago—embrace the central commitments of our constitutional philosophy. (Indeed, the current level of public anger is high in significant part because commitments that are so meaningful to most of us are so clearly under assault.) Most of us (culture warriors excepted) have adopted and internalized the "live and let live" beliefs that animate our Bill of Rights, and that attitude has greatly facilitated our relationships with our fellow citizens. What urban and progressive activists criticize is an extreme economic individualism that is no longer consistent with the realities of many urban lives.

This new sensibility is certainly not an embrace of socialism, nor (political rhetoric notwithstanding) is it an indiscriminate "bleeding heart" approach to urban problems. Instead, it is a recognition that the current social contract is simply not working for large numbers of Americans, and that (Calvinist worldviews to the contrary notwithstanding) the fault rarely lies with those who are being left behind. Most poor Americans work forty hours a week or more. Unexpected or catastrophic medical expenses cause over half of the nation's personal bankruptcies. Inadequate public schools in our poorest neighborhoods perpetuate cycles of poverty. The lack of reliable public transportation contributes to congestion and poor air quality for all of us; for those unable to afford a car (or increasingly, the gas to power it), it makes every transaction difficult and prevents access to potential jobs. This nation's poor face systemic problems that defy easy admonitions by more-privileged (and isolated) Americans to "just work harder" or to "pull yourself up by your own bootstraps." When people wake up every morning to a system that does not work for them, does not respond to their efforts or accommodate their most basic needs, it should not be surprising that they don't face the new day with an abundance of trust.

If we truly want to address the issue of trust in America, there are two things we need to do. First, we need to restore integrity to our government and recommit ourselves to the US Constitution and the rule of law. That will also require that we address the deficiencies in our electoral system and ensure that the American ideal of "one person, one vote" is descriptive rather than aspirational.

Second, we need to listen to the inhabitants of the urban archipelago, who are telling us that complex, densely populated communities can no longer depend upon tribal and individual responses to social needs. We need to revisit the American social contract, and thoroughly overhaul our frayed and inadequate social safety net. That does not mean abandoning our commitment to limited government (although it may mean refusing to equate "limited" government with "small" government). We still need to ask the age-old question: what should government do? But the answer—as those in the urban archipelago know—must include government solutions to problems that individuals and the market can't solve. Government, after all, is a tool; it is the mechanism we use when collective action is necessary. People of good faith will debate the circumstances justifying state action, and they will debate the nature of the action to be taken. That is a necessary debate—and one that is considerably overdue.

Diversity is not our enemy. Americans don't need to attend the same church, vote for the same politicians, or enjoy the same entertainments. We don't need to be the same color or trace our ancestors to the same continent. What we do need is a renewed sense that we are all participants in the same national dialogue, and that we share a common commitment to the American Idea. We also—desperately—need trustworthy, transparent, accountable governing institutions that will respect the Constitution and individual rights and that will respond appropriately to our changing social needs.

NOTES

1. Michael Kosfeld, M. Heinrichs, P. J. Zak, U. Fischbacher, and E. Fehr, "Oxytocin Increases Trust in Humans," *Nature* 435, no. 2 (2005): 673–76.

2. Jan Delhey and Kenneth Newton, "Who Trusts?: The Origins of Social Trust in Seven Societies," *European Societies* 5, no. 2 (2003): 93–137.

3. Ibid.

4. There is a good deal of research suggesting that high levels of social capital are associated with better government; the open question, of course, is which came first—does social capital lead to good, or at least better, government, or does good government create social capital?

5. Delhey and Newton, "Who Trusts?"

6. Ibid.

7. Carles Boix and Daniel N. Posner, "Social Capital: Explaining Its Origins and Effects on Government Performance," *British Journal of Political Science* 28, no. 4 (1998): 687.

8. As Nicholas Lemann dryly noted (in a 1996 article titled "Kicking in Groups"), the opposite of Putnam's theory would be that the decline in "civic virtue" was largely confined to the decade 1965–1975, when both crime and divorce rates rose dramatically, and that the "overwhelming social and moral problem in American life is instead the disastrous condition of poor neighborhoods. . . . Rather than assume, with Putnam, that such essential public goods as safety, decent housing, and good education can be generated only from within a community, we could assume that they might be provided from without—by government" (*Atlantic Monthly* 277, no. 4, p. 26).

9. Marc Hooghe, Tim Reeskens, Dietlind Stolle, and Ann Trapper, "Ethnic Diversity, Trust and Ethnocentrism and Europe: A Multilevel Analysis of 21 European Countries," paper presented at the 102nd American Political Science Association Annual Meeting, Philadelphia 2006.

10. Margery Austin Turner and Julie Fenderson, "Under-

standing Diverse Neighborhoods in an Era of Demographic Change," Fannie Mae Foundation & Urban Institute, June 2006.

11. Emma Lazarus is the poet who penned the famous words inscribed at the foot of the Statue of Liberty: "Give me your tired, your poor, your huddled masses yearning to breathe free. . . . I lift my lamp beside the Golden Door."

12. "The Urban Archipelago: It's the Cities, Stupid," *Stranger* 14, no. 9 (2004).

13. Ibid.

14. Ibid.

15. Ibid.

Chapter 7

BEING ALL WE CAN BE

Three Modest Proposals

So—what can we conclude from the somewhat disparate strands of the preceding discussion? What do we know about social trust and diversity, and what can we do about what we know?

To begin with, we can be reasonably certain America has a trust problem. Not only is the national mood angry, cynical, and distrustful, but in areas where there is greater diversity and among populations that have historically been less trustful, Putnam's research shows that our already low trust levels are even lower. Both the "trust deficit" and the "trust gap" threaten our ability to generate social capital and are barriers to our ability to come together in order to solve national problems and advance American interests.

On the other hand, we have—if we will recognize and use it—an important tool to deal with our present situation: a vision of America. That vision, shaped by a governing structure that was based not upon trust but upon the *trustworthiness* of our governing institutions (at most, ours is a system we might call "trust but verify"), is an indelible feature of our national culture and a priceless gift from our Founding Fathers.

The founders were highly skeptical of centralized power, and so our various checks and balances were put in place to create and ensure a *trustworthy* government, a government where the built-in structure of checks and balances would substitute, or compensate, for the all-too-predictable fallibility of many of the individuals who would eventually hold public office. Most Americans still cling to that vision of a trustworthy, even admirable, government and a citizenry that draws its unity not from a common identity, but from a common devotion to American constitutional values.

With respect to immigration, history reminds us that we've been here before and emerged better for it. The story of America has been etched in a constant series of encounters with newcomers who don't look like the (ever-changing) rest of us. We have frequently behaved badly in the course of those encounters, but in most cases, over time, we have come to regard those others as a legitimate part of the American tapestry. Who "we" are and what "we" look like has changed and evolved accordingly.

In addition to these facts—historical and descriptive—the preceding chapters have set out what I believe to be reasonable assumptions about the reasons for the current national mood. Our governing institutions are not operating as they were intended to. The Bush administration's assault on our constitutional system in pursuit of unchecked power has been intense, and its operation of the various governmental agencies Americans rely on has too often proved to be not just untrustworthy but incompetent and unreliable.[1] Administration policies have eroded our already frayed social safety net, and dramatically increased the distance between the rich and well connected and the rest of us.

Every day brings new revelations of corruption or crisis, not just in our government, but in our other important institutions as well. We are having yet another national argument about immigration—legal and not—and we continue to grapple with the issue of race. Religious fundamentalists challenge our efforts to extend equal civil rights to gays and lesbians. And all of these problems, and hundreds more, are endlessly debated, recycled, and dissected on millions of blogs and Web sites—thanks to the ubiquity of modern communications, it is virtually impossible to avoid daily reports and warnings about dangers and failures at home or abroad. And all of this is happening at a time of rapid and irreversible globalization and accelerated social change—a time of social transition that (as I have argued in prior chapters) has also changed the very character of the trust we need. American society has become too complex, our population has become too large and too urban, to allow us to depend upon the kinds of interpersonal and small-scale generalized trust in the motives and behaviors of others that served small towns and homogeneous communities in the past.

In this time of transition, the trust we need most is *institutional*. Rather than asking survey respondents whether they believe that "most people" can be trusted, we should be asking whether our collective agencies—our *social mechanisms*—can be trusted. As one scholar notes,

> Diversity is a well-established fact of contemporary life that is more likely to increase than decrease over time, and many interactions in modern societies inevitably take place in a large scale. It therefore seems more productive to examine how and why diversity and group size impact cooperation, and to consider how to mitigate negative impacts and take

advantage of positive ones, than to debate the abstract merits of diversity or to pine away for simpler times that may or may not have been superior to modernity.[2]

Barros concludes—as I have—that we have no alternative but to look to our legal structures, which inevitably shape human interactions, to create the reciprocity we require in an ever more heterogeneous world. And the most important of those legal structures, obviously, is government.

OUR NECESSARY GOVERNMENT

Ronald Reagan was fond of saying that government isn't the solution, it's the problem. In reality, it's both. Societies require governments—no matter what the anarchists claim—and the more complex the society, the more pressing the need and the more extensive the government. It is when government does not function properly—when it intrudes into areas that are inappropriate for government intervention, when it violates the terms of our original social contract, or when it performs its necessary and proper functions in an incompetent or corrupt manner—that it becomes a problem.

In America today, even the most libertarian citizens need to be able to trust that appropriate regulatory agencies are policing the bankers from whom they obtain their home mortgages, the brokers who sell them investments, the doctors who diagnose and treat their illnesses. We all need to trust government agencies to inspect our food and drink and medicines, and to ensure that the toys we are importing don't contain unsafe levels of lead. We need to have confidence that FEMA will assist effectively when disaster strikes, that the CDC will be alert for signs of bird flu or SARS, that the SEC will monitor the accuracy of reports issued by the companies we invest in, and the FDIC will insure the savings we deposit in our local bank. Without a level of public confidence in these and literally hundreds of other agencies, the economy will cease to function, and life in the urban areas where most of us live will be impossible to sustain.

Restoring our faith in the competence and constitutionality of our governing institutions is vitally important, because there is no other single institution that we can trust to act as society's umpire. To risk repeating the lessons of Economics 101, government steps in when there has been a "market failure," when individuals and voluntary associations cannot or will not meet a particular need. It is important to recognize that the character of market failures and the identity of the tasks the private sector cannot perform has changed over time, and will continue to change in response to the ever-evolving complexities of modern life. People don't keep their money in cash under mattresses any more (if we ever did). As individuals, we can't even walk in and examine the books of our (no longer local) bank. As individuals, we can't even require that the bank make its books public for inspection. Individuals can't detect the bacterial count of the foods we buy at the grocery. We can't even calculate the nutritional value of that food—we must depend upon the accuracy of the (governmentally required) label. We certainly can't handle our own air traffic control duties. In so many respects, we are far less independent and far more interdependent than our farming ancestors—if we lose our jobs, most of us don't have our own vegetable gardens and chickens to fall back on. Contemporary Americans need collective mechanisms through which these and hundreds of other similar problems and tasks can be addressed by accountable, disinterested agencies. And it should go without saying that we need to have confidence that these collective agencies are not favoring some citizens over others without just cause; we need to trust that those who manage them are not trading public services for personal or political gain. In short, we need to know that they are *trustworthy*.

America needs competent government agencies that will do what private citizens, businesses, and nonprofit organizations increasingly cannot—agencies that we can trust to discharge their obligations in a manner consistent with the rule of law. We will inevitably disagree about the need for this or that government program, or about the criteria by which we will evaluate official competence, but government itself is a necessity, and robust government—like diversity—is and will increasingly be a fact of our collective lives. Our choice is not between vestigial and substantial government; it is between competent, constitutional government and government run amok.

GOVERNMENT AND THE TRUST PROBLEM

American government is a significant contributor both to our sour national mood and the so-called trust gap found by researchers. As I have argued in chapters 4 and 5, in the first case, the problem is what government is doing; in the second, the problem is what government *isn't* doing.

What government is doing wrong (and what the public believes government is doing wrong) is a major contributor to the sullen, angry public mood that we have experienced over the past few years, and one of the things government is doing wrong is failing to listen to the voice of its citizens.[3] There is, as previously noted, a growing body of research on the importance of "voice."[4] People who feel that their concerns are discounted or unheard build up enormous amounts of resentment. When we look at the significance of voice to the democratic process, studies suggest that people who support the losing side in an election that they believe was fair—an election where they were able to get their message out, where they feel confident that the votes were properly counted, and so on—are much more likely to experience the result as fair and are willing to accept the loss. (This research helps to explain the bitterness with which so many Democrats responded to the election of 2000—when the Democrat actually won the popular vote, and where the constitutional process for resolving the Florida vote was short-circuited by the Supreme Court. The perception of irregularity in the 2000 election then fed a certain amount of paranoia in 2004, when the presidential election was also dogged by accusations of irregularity.)

It isn't only the electoral process. As we have seen, American citizens are subjected to an exponentially increasing daily diet of news reports, blog posts, talk radio diatribes, and television roundtables. A huge number of these publications and broadcasts focus upon accusations of government lawlessness and ineptitude, either by making charges of wrongdoing or by defending the targets against those charges. Over the past six or seven years, the allegations of government misconduct and malfeasance have gotten steadily more serious and more credible. Poll after poll confirms that large and growing majorities of Americans feel the country is "on the wrong track." Until we fix our broken governing structures, and restore American confidence in their competence, fairness, and impartiality, the national mood will not improve.

Fixing what government is doing wrong is necessary, but it isn't sufficient. A renewed faith in our leadership and our constitutional system will undoubtedly improve general levels of trust, but improved governing institutions alone will not address the trust gap. For that, we need to take a hard look at our inadequate, tattered social safety net.

As we have seen, available research strongly suggests that insecurity and anxiety contribute significantly to generalized distrust. The impact of anxiety shows most clearly in the area of public safety, but it is inextricably intertwined with the absence of a social safety net.[5] One pertinent example: Many observers have wondered about the difference in levels of gun violence between Canada and the United States. Here are two nations with similar populations and legal antecedents. Canadians watch American television. Gun ownership is widespread in both countries. Yet the incidence of homicide in Canada is nowhere near the level in America. Comparative research on crime suggests that we should look for an explanation of the difference in Canada's much more reliable social safety net.[6] The availability of social welfare programs reduces anxiety, and reductions in anxiety translate to reductions in crimes of violence and passion.

The connection between poverty and crime has been widely documented, as has the ameliorating effect of public assistance. In "The Truly Disadvantaged, Public Assistance, and Crime," Lance Hannon and James Defronzo concluded that "the prevalence of resource deprivation had significantly less effect on crimes rates in areas with higher levels of welfare assistance."[7] Other scholars have found that levels of lethal violence are higher in countries with weak collective institutions of social protection.[8] The lack of social support correlates with higher crime levels and levels of general stress and anomie.

In our modern, highly mobile society and our densely populated metropolitan areas, people no longer rely upon extended families or long-time neighbors to help out when the kids get sick or the car breaks down. The days when neighbors could be counted on to help pick the crops or raise the barn are long gone, even in farming communities. Nor would most Americans have the ability or time to reciprocate in kind if their neighbors did these things. Because we can no longer routinely depend on people we know to provide assistance when we need it, that social support must be supplied by our collective institutions—and that includes government social insurance programs.

As social historian Stephanie Coontz has pointed out, this

tricting, allocation of electoral votes, and voting by mail—
would be a major step toward making our elections more trustworthy. Bipartisan redistricting would return us to a system
where voters choose their political representatives, rather than
the one we currently have, where politicians essentially choose
their voters. Allocating the electoral vote to more closely
mirror the popular vote would give voice to those whom the
current system effectively disenfranchises. And conducting
elections by mail would get rid of the mixed messages we currently send to voters when we simultaneously conduct get-out-
the-vote efforts while imposing substantial barriers to their
ability to cast a ballot. Fairer and more trustworthy election
practices would also be an important first step toward
achieving Modest Proposal Number Two.

MODEST PROPOSAL NUMBER TWO: RESTORE GOVERNMENTAL ACCOUNTABILITY

There are two kinds of governmental accountability: political
and constitutional. Whether either or both will be addressed in
the next few years will depend upon the new administration
and the composition of the incoming Congress. Many of the
prescriptions here are self-evident, and widely recognized.

The process of appointing people to manage government
agencies needs to be depoliticized. One of the reasons for the
original creation of the civil service was recognition that many
functions of government require expertise—that passing a
political litmus test is no substitute for competence. The EPA
needs scientists who understand environmental issues; the
FDA needs researchers whose dedication to public health is
greater than their political or religious ideologies. FEMA needs
managers with demonstrated competence in disaster relief,
and the Department of Justice should be staffed by talented
lawyers who are actually devoted to promoting justice as our

legal system has defined that term, rather than to partisan agendas. If we are ever going to restore trust in our government, we need to reassure the public that the people employed by its myriad agencies are there because they know what they are doing, not just because they have political connections.

Conflict-of-interest laws, and the laws regulating lobbyists and lobbying activity, need to be revisited and their provisions updated and tightened. We may never be able to squeeze the influence of money out of the electoral system (successive efforts to do so have largely failed, and several have had unfortunate unintended consequences),[16] but we can and should strengthen the oversight mechanisms that are in place to prevent outright corruption of the sort that became almost commonplace during the Bush administration. The list of Bush officials who were actually indicted or convicted is appallingly long: Scooter Libby, Vice President Dick Cheney's chief of staff, who resigned after being indicted for obstruction of justice, perjury, and making false statements; Lester Crawford, the FDA commissioner who resigned after pleading guilty to conflict of interest and making false statements; David Safavian, the former head of the Office of Federal Procurement Policy at the Office of Management and Budget, who was convicted of lying to ethics officials and Senate investigators about his dealings with lobbyist Jack Abramoff; Roger Stillwell, a desk officer at the Interior Department, who pled guilty for failing to report payoffs from Jack Abramoff; Darleen Druyun, a senior contracting official with the US Air Force, who was sentenced to nine months in prison for her role in the Boeing tanker lease scandal; John Korsmo, the chairman of the Federal Housing Finance Board who pled guilty to lying to the Senate and an inspector general about invitations issued to a list of presidents of FHFB-regulated banks to a fundraiser for his friend's congressional campaign (the invitations listed Korsmo as the "Special Guest"); and P. Trey Sunderland III, the chief of Geriatric Psychiatry at the National Institute of Mental Health, who pled guilty to a criminal conflict of interest charge for failing to report $500,000 received from Pfizer, Inc. And these are just the appointees who abused their official positions—the list doesn't include the White House domestic policy advisor who was convicted of shoplifting at Target, or the Homeland Security official who was convicted in a sex scandal. It also doesn't include a much longer list of people who resigned because they were facing investigations. To belabor the obvious, when every week brings new reports of wrongdoing, trust in government suffers.

Most important of all, we must reverse the erosion of our constitutional checks and balances. Power is the ultimate aphrodisiac, however, and there are no guarantees that the incoming administration will be able to resist the temptation to retain the extraordinary—and extralegal—powers that the Bush administration accrued. The Congress has been slow to assert its prerogatives as an equal branch of government, even after the 2006 midterm elections gave control to the Democrats, but that is where true reform should begin. A bipartisan commission, similar to the 9/11 Commission or the older Church Committee, should investigate the constitutional breaches that have occurred and should issue a comprehensive report detailing the "State of the Constitution." If there are persuasive arguments for ignoring treaties, for holding detainees without due process, for suspending habeas corpus, for spying on American citizens without the approval of the FISA Court, or for any of the other actions that are widely believed to have violated the rule of law, those arguments should be publicly made and debated. If they have merit, Congress should indicate its agreement by resolution or legislation as appropriate. If they do not, the individuals who violated the public trust must be sanctioned, and the sanctions must be meaningful. Many highly credible and reputable observers have made a strong case for impeaching George W. Bush and Dick Cheney. For whatever reasons—political or strategic—Congress has failed to institute impeachment proceedings, but that should not mean that we simply drop the inquiry when they leave office. There must be a comprehensive accounting, and appropriate action, civil or criminal, as appropriate. The American public is entitled to no less.

Above all, these debates must be public. When government acts covertly, when its decisions are secret and its actions secretive, citizens are right to be distrustful and cynical. When our elected officials announce, in essence, that they are exempt from the rules that apply to the rest of us, what they are really saying is that we have abandoned the rule of law. They are telling us that constitutional checks and balances are too confining and will no longer be obeyed, and furthermore, that we have no right to information about the decisions that they are making—that we should simply trust that they are good individuals who will do what is best for us. That—as everyone who passed high school government knows—is not the American Way.

Whether we can reign government in again and make it obedient to constitutional norms remains to be seen. But we absolutely won't be able to do it unless we can revitalize civic education. American constitutional illiteracy is at the root of much that is wrong with our government. It fosters distrust: if you don't know what the rules are, how do you really know whether they are being broken? If, as I have argued, it is allegiance to the American Idea that identifies American citizens, if it is adherence to a particular vision of human liberty and individual rights that creates unity from our diversity, then at least some degree of constitutional competence and knowledge of that American Idea is critical to our identity as a nation. In other words, if we are (in Todd Gitlin's phrase) a voluntary country, it behooves us to know what we are volunteering for and why. Americans will always argue at the margins; we will disagree about the application of this or that principle to new and different situations. But we need to agree on the basics. At the very least, we need to know what those basics are. And if my own students are an indication, we have a lot of work to do.

MODEST PROPOSAL NUMBER THREE: SOCIAL RECIPROCITY

What I have been calling "institutional" trust can also be thought of as social reciprocity, the comfort and security that come from knowing that if X occurs, institution Y will be there to help. That's where the social safety net comes in.

In neighborhoods where people live under constant stress, crime increases. Increased crime adds to the stress and insecurity. If anxiety and insecurity erode social capital, programs that ameliorate insecurity can only strengthen it. By far the most pressing issue for most working-class and middle-class Americans today is the escalating cost and declining availability of healthcare. The problems created by our current patchwork nonsystem (or, as a Health Administration student once told me, we don't really have a healthcare *system* in America, we have a healthcare *industry*) distort our economy and threaten other important social welfare programs. (There is, as Paul Krugman and others have reminded us, no Social Security crisis—it is a Medicare crisis.)

There are major problems plaguing our healthcare system: mounting costs, the growing number of people who are uninsured, declining and/or uneven quality of care, and the growing gap between the level of care available to the affluent and that available to lower-income Americans. The National Coalition on Health Care has noted that these problems are interrelated: efforts to expand coverage are made more difficult by rising healthcare prices; at the same time, reduced access to care among the uninsured actually drives up costs, because the uninsured don't get routine preventive care and typically seek medical attention only when they are much sicker. They are also more likely to seek that care in the most expensive settings—hospital emergency rooms and emergency clinics. It doesn't help that, due to its patchwork nature, our system does not provide sufficient incentives for broad and highly cost-effective *public health* initiatives to combat environmental and other causes of health problems and thus prevent many illnesses.

Poll after poll confirms that large majorities of Americans want a fairer, more uniform system. A 2007 survey by ABC News and the *Washington Post* found that Americans by a 2–1 margin prefer a universal health insurance program over the current employer-based system.[17] Similar results were reported by a CBS/*New York Times* poll: "Americans think the U.S. health care system is in need of major repairs. . . . Nine out of 10 say the system needs at least fundamental changes, including 36 percent who favor a complete overhaul."[18] The strength of these numbers is surprising, given the acrimonious nature of discussion about the proper role of government in our lives generally and in the healthcare system in particular.

The United States spends far more per capita for healthcare than any other country—more than twice as much as our nearest competitor—yet we are routinely ranked thirty-sixth or thirty-seventh by the World Health Organization. A recent Commonwealth Fund–supported study comparing preventable deaths in nineteen countries ranked the United States dead last.[19] Given the persistent public support for reform, and the fact that we spend so much more and get so much less than other Western industrialized countries, America's dogged refusal to change is routinely attributed to our ideological predisposition to limited government and especially to the existence of powerful players with entrenched interests in the status quo. Any comprehensive reform will have to confront a medical/industrial/insurance complex that has billions of dollars a year at stake: early in 2008, healthcare spending passed two *trillion* dollars annually.[20]

What is ironic about this state of affairs is that the government is massively involved in healthcare already—but its involvement is unfocused, inefficient, and often counterproductive. Some form of single-payer health system would be better for the economy, as well as for our social and physical health, and it would go far toward plugging the trust gap.

National healthcare would mean increased economic development and job creation. The business sector currently expends an amount in excess of its net profits on health insurance for employees. The cost of health insurance is the single largest "drag" on new job creation. For companies that can afford to offer health insurance (a rapidly dwindling number), negotiating and administering those benefits, and complying with government regulations attendant to them, consumes untold hours of HR time as well. (It should be noted that medical offices also spend considerable sums on personnel whose sole job is confirming insurance coverage, complying with insurer regulations, submitting claims, and collecting amounts due.) Smaller companies—the engines of economic growth—are often unable to offer benefits, putting them at a competitive disadvantage for good employees. If health coverage was decoupled from employment, employers could hire more workers and could increase wages by some percentage of the amount currently being paid for insurance. Freed of healthcare costs, American businesses would be better able to compete in an increasingly global economy.

Despite the scare tactics employed by insurance and pharmaceutical companies, research suggests that the additional tax revenues needed to provide everyone with basic coverage would be minimal. Few Americans are aware of the magnitude of current government expenditures on health; government at all levels already spends huge amounts for health through

Medicare, Medicaid, and other federal programs; through benefits for public employees (healthcare for public university professors and staff, police and firefighters, public school teachers, and numerous other federal, state, and municipal employees is already paid for with tax dollars); by funding medical and drug research; and through support for public hospitals. Government agencies currently pay 47 percent of all direct healthcare costs, a percentage that will exceed 50 percent by 2017.[21] When indirect payments—health insurance for millions of government employees, federal grants for medical research and development, and so on—are added in, national, state, and local governments already pay between 60 and 70 percent of all US health costs, and the programs through which they do so are incredibly wasteful and duplicative. A single-payer system would offer enormous economies of scale.

A uniform health system would save significant amounts just by standardizing paperwork and administrative procedures (it is estimated that as much as 30 percent of US healthcare costs are administrative). Insurers and drug manufacturers currently spend enormous amounts on marketing and advertising, costs that would be rendered largely unnecessary in a single-payer system. By providing more effective public health and prevention services and providing routine care, the costs we incur as a result of delayed treatment would be reduced. (Costs decline when people are able to access routine medical care soon after the onset of symptoms, rather than visiting far more expensive emergency rooms when they can no longer ignore the problem.) Huge savings could be effected by negotiating with drug manufacturers and other medical vendors for lower prices.[22] Cost controls would also be enhanced by eliminating the practice of cost-shifting by hospitals (where those with insurance pay prices that have been inflated in order to cover the costs that cannot be recovered from those without). Individuals would save money too, even assuming their taxes increased to cover their health benefits. Premiums for family health insurance policies are currently averaging over $12,000 per year, and even those fortunate enough to work for employers who still provide coverage are paying larger shares of those annual premiums, as global competition forces employers to shift costs to their employees. Auto and homeowners' insurance premiums are artificially inflated, because the underwriting has to take the costs of medical care into account. Those premiums would decline. And perhaps most important: the considerable—and growing—number of citizens who are uninsured would no longer risk losing everything to illness or accident.

If all citizens had at least basic health coverage, we would also see a decline in the human and social costs associated with our current, dysfunctional system. In January, the Urban Institute reported that 137,000 preventable deaths had occurred between 2000 and 2006 solely because those who died lacked health insurance. "The absence of health insurance creates a range of consequences, including lower quality of life, increased morbidity and mortality, and higher financial burdens."[23] Over 50 percent of personal bankruptcies are attributable to medical bills; those bankruptcies cost businesses millions of dollars every year, and are a drag on the economy. Employees with preexisting conditions would no longer be chained to jobs they dislike. Absenteeism could be expected to decline. Studies also suggest that violent crime rates decline as social safety nets increase. None of these outcomes is quantifiable, but their impact is likely to be substantial. Most important for the purpose of restoring public trust and addressing the trust gap, a system offering basic health coverage to all citizens would go far to alleviate the high levels of anxiety that so many middle-class and working Americans live with on a day-to-day basis.[24]

WHY THESE PROPOSALS?

If government integrity is an important prerequisite to institutional and generalized trust, the logic behind my first two "modest proposals" is self-evident. If Americans need to trust that government "of the people, by the people" is genuinely the choice of the people, election reforms aimed at increasing the responsiveness and transparency of our elections are rather clearly relevant to that goal.

Integrity is not simply the absence of outright corruption, important though that is. It is conformity with our national legal framework and fidelity to the rule of law. In order to earn back public confidence, our government must keep faith with the promises of our constituent documents, especially the United States Constitution. Abuses of power create anxiety and distrust in any country; when they occur in a nation committed to limited state authority and the rule of law, those abuses are even more threatening.

A proposal for national healthcare, on the other hand, may seem oddly inconsistent with an argument based upon fidelity to the idea of limited government. Properly understood, however, the argument for limiting the power of the state is not necessarily an argument for limiting the scope of all government activity. Sometimes it will be; other times it won't. The pertinent question is: Is this an activity that can and should be left to the private sector—that is, are we dealing with a good that the market can provide? The answer to that question will change over time, as the practical realities of particular human endeavors change. (It used to be taken for granted that the government should deliver the mail, for example; with the advent of e-mail and private services like UPS and Federal Express, the propriety and extent of a government postal service is being reexamined. For good or ill, the privatization movement has called government service delivery into question in a number of areas. At the same time, and often for sound reasons, government has moved into areas not remotely contemplated by the nation's founders; protecting the environment is only one example.) The American preference for market mechanisms is generally well founded; the free market has created enormous wealth in which we all share, and in areas where the market is working, we would be well advised to limit government to its proper role as regulator and as guarantor of the level playing field.

Three questions are relevant to an analysis of the propriety of governmentally provided healthcare. First, is healthcare more like public safety or is it more like a consumer good—that is, is it something to which all Americans should be entitled by virtue of our membership in the American community, or should we continue our current practice of rationing medical care on the same basis as we ration automobiles and washing machines—on the basis of ability to pay? The second question is whether the market is currently providing adequate medical services at affordable prices. And the third question is whether a change to universal access provided by government will make America a stronger, better, more trusting country.

People of good will can argue whether healthcare should be a right or a privilege—that is essentially a moral argument. But whatever our conclusions on that score, the answers to the second and third question seem—to me at least—dispositive. The market has not provided healthcare for a long time; government is providing it (albeit in a highly inefficient and unnecessarily expensive fashion). Rhetoric about the promise and/or perils of "socialized medicine" are entirely beside the point, because we already have socialized medicine. Unfortunately, we have socialized our system through private insurance companies, giving us the worst of both worlds. Our current nonsystem has all of the drawbacks attributed to government provision and none of the efficiencies.

Would universal access to healthcare make us a better nation? There is much evidence to suggest that it would. If the trust gap, in particular, is attributable in some significant measure to fear, anxiety, and insecurity, a better social safety net can only ameliorate it.

Let me be very clear about what I am saying—and what I am most definitely *not* saying. The sorts of distrust found by social scientists like Putnam are certainly not all grounded in lack of access to healthcare. Nor can they all be attributed to the misdeeds and misguided policies of the Bush administration. There are a number of social, cognitive, and psychological reasons why it can be more difficult for people from diverse backgrounds to trust each other and behave reciprocally. It is harder for most of us to work with people who have very different perspectives, who bring different experiences and social norms to the public conversation. Researchers sometimes explain those difficulties as higher "transaction costs."[25] It simply requires more effort to understand each other, for one thing. And we cannot overlook the detrimental effects of divisive political strategies: the growing use of what political scientists call "wedge" or "culture war" issues, or the fear levels stoked by color-coded terror alerts and frequent references to "Islamic terrorists."

I am certainly not suggesting that passing election reforms and enacting national health insurance will somehow obviate all of the pressures and life experiences that make us distrustful. Instead, I am making a far more modest claim: that by strengthening our collective governing institutions, and providing all citizens with basic social security, we will be far more likely—and better equipped—to do the hard work necessary to overcome barriers, and to understand and work with each other.

sive, and for good reason. As Michael Moore's film *Sicko* illustrated to a wide audience, insurance companies go to great lengths to deny coverage or disallow expenses. Although Moore is frequently dismissed as an agitator, there is a wealth of evidence available to confirm his basic assertions.

25. Barros, "Group Size, Heterogeneity, and Prosocial Behavior."

26. Michael Hais and Morley Winograd, "Millennials Are about to Give American Politics an Extreme Makeover," *Huffington Post,* February 7, 2006, http://www.huffingtonpost.com/michael-hais -and-morley-winograd/millennials-are-about-to-_b_85556.html.

27. Maureen Dowd, "Voting for a Smile," *New York Times*, January 6, 2008.

AFTERWORD

Recovering America

Most countries have gone through periods of turmoil, corruption, or worse. I know of none that have escaped episodes of poor—sometimes disastrous—leadership. And as anyone who follows the news knows, democracies are hardly immune; the electoral process is no guarantee that you won't get leaders who are ill equipped to govern. All governments are human enterprises, and like all human enterprises, they will have their ups and downs. In the United States, however, the consequences of the "down" periods are potentially more serious than in more homogeneous nations, precisely because this is a country based not upon identity but upon covenant. Americans do not share a single ethnicity, religion, or race. *We never have.* We don't share a worldview. We don't even fully share a culture. What we do share is a set of values, and when those whom we elect betray those values, we don't just lose trust. We lose a critical part of what it is that makes us Americans.

Policy prescriptions and ten-point plans (or three-part "Modest Proposals") are all well and good, but at the end of the day, our public policies must be aligned with and supportive of our most fundamental values, and the people we elect must demonstrate that they understand, respect, and live up to those values.

As we have seen, the word *values* means different things to different people. In the wake of the agonizingly close 2004 presidential election, pundits told us that voters had come out on November 4 to vote for values. What they meant by *values*—opposition to reproductive choice and equal rights for gays and lesbians, and nationalistic jingoism masquerading as patriotism—was the antithesis of the American values most of us really do care about. Let me be quite explicit about what I believe to be genuine American values—values that have been shaped by our constitutional culture, values that are shared by the millions of Americans who have been dismayed and dispirited by the revelations of the past eight years. They are the values that infuse the Declaration of Independence, the Constitution, and the Bill of Rights—the values that are absolutely central to the American Idea:

- Americans believe in justice and civil liberties—understood as equal treatment and fair play for all citizens, whether or not they look like us, and whether or not we agree with them or like them or approve of their reading materials, religious beliefs, or other life choices.
- Americans believe in the rule of law. And we believe that *no one* is above the law—most emphatically including those who run our government. We believe the same rules should apply to everyone who is in the same circumstances, that allowing interest groups to "buy" more

favorable rules or other special treatment with campaign contributions, political horse-trading, or outright bribery is un-American.

- Americans believe in our inalienable right to speak our minds, even when—perhaps *especially* when—we disagree with the government. We understand that dissent can be the highest form of patriotism, just as mindless affirmation of the choices made by those in power can wreak untold damage on the country. Those who care about America enough to speak out against policies they believe to be wrong or corrupt are not only exercising their rights as citizens, they are discharging their most sacred civic responsibilities.

- Americans believe that when politicians play to the worst of our fears and prejudices, using "wedge issues" to marginalize immigrants, or gays, or blacks, or "East Coast liberals" (a time-honored code word for *Jews*) in the pursuit of political advantage, they are being un-American and immoral.

- Americans believe in the importance of reason, the need for tolerance, and respect for evidence, including scientific evidence. We may go "off the reservation" from time to time, especially when the weight of the evidence points to results we don't like, but eventually, Americans will place reason and compromise above denial and intransigence in the conduct of our collective affairs.

- Americans believe, to use the language of the nation's Founding Fathers, in "a decent respect for the opinions of mankind" (even European mankind).

- Finally, Americans believe in the true heartland of this country, which is not to be found on a map. The real heartland is made up of all the Americans who struggle every day to provide for their families, dig deep into their pockets to help the less fortunate, and understand their religions to require goodwill and loving kindness. The men and women who make up that heartland understand that self-righteousness is the enemy of righteousness. They know that the way you play the game is more important, in the end, than whether you win or lose. And they know that, in America, the ends don't justify the means.

Americans' ability to trust one another depends upon our ability to keep faith with these values.

Life in a liberal democratic polity is never going to be harmonious. Harmony, after all, wasn't the American Idea. Despite the dreams of the communitarians, we aren't all going to share the same *telos*; at most, we will have what John Rawls called an "overlapping consensus."[1] In a country that celebrates individual rights and respects individual liberty, there will always be dissent, differences of opinion, and struggles for power. But there are different kinds of discord, and they aren't all equal. When we argue from within the constitutional culture—when we argue about the proper application of the American Idea to new situations or to previously marginalized populations—we strengthen our bonds and learn how to bridge our differences. When our divisions and debates are between powerful forces that want to rewrite our most basic rules and citizens without the wherewithal to enforce them, we undermine the American Idea and erode social trust.

At the end of the day, diversity (however we want to define it) is not the problem. And that's a good thing, because the fact is that increasing diversity is inescapable. The real issue is whether it is too late to restore our institutional infrastructure and make our government trustworthy again, whether we can once again reinvigorate the American Idea and make it work in a brave new world characterized by nearly instantaneous communications, unprecedented human mobility, and the twin challenges of climate change and international terrorism. There are hopeful signs, but the jury is still out.

NOTE

1. John Rawls, *Political Liberalism* (New York: Columbia University Press, 1993).

BIBLIOGRAPHY

2000 US Census, US Census Bureau.

CBS/*New York Times* Poll. September 14–16, 2007.

"Debt Load for City Is Becoming a Key Issue." *Indianapolis Star*, June 29, 1999.

"A Mayor Shows Gore's Team the Way." *Washington Post*, August 25, 1993.

"Privatization Run Amuck." *Indianapolis Star*, August 30, 1994.

"The Urban Archipelago: It's the Cities, Stupid." *Stranger* 14, no. 9 (2004).

Alonso-Zaldivar, Ricardo. "Democratic Hopefuls Agree on Medicare as a Healthcare Model." *Los Angeles Times*, January 21, 2008.

Arneil, Barbara. *Diverse Communities: The Problem with Social Capital.* Cambridge: Cambridge University Press, 2006.

Aulakh, Sundeep. "The Transformation of the UK State: Rolling Back or Rolling Out?" Paper presented at the Transatlantic Policy Consortium Conference, Speyer, Germany, 2003.

Backman, E. V., and S. R. Smith. "Healthy Organizations, Unhealthy Communities?" *Nonprofit Management and Leadership* 10, no. 4 (2000): 355–73.

Barros, B. "Group Size, Heterogeneity, and Prosocial Behavior: Designing Legal Structures to Facilitate Cooperation in a Diverse Society." Widener Law School Legal Studies Research Paper No. 08-12. http://ssrn.com/abstract = 1015188.

Beiner, Ronald. "What Liberalism Means." *Social Philosophy and Policy* 13, no. 1 (1996): 190–206.

Bellah, Robert N. *Habits of the Heart: Individualism and Commitment in American Life.* Berkeley: University of California Press, 1985.

———. "The Protestant Structure of American Culture: Multiculture or Monoculture." *Hedgehog Review* 4 (2002): 7–28.

Berger, Peter L. *The Sacred Canopy.* Garden City, NY: Doubleday, 1967.

Berger, Peter L., and B. Berger. "The Blueing of America." *New Republic* 183 (1969).

Blumberg, L. J., and J. Holahan. "Do Individual Mandates Matter?" *Timely Analysis of Immediate Health Policy Issues* (Urban Institute, January 30, 2008).

Boaz, David. *Libertarianism: A Primer.* New York: Free Press, 1997.

Boix, Carles, and Daniel N. Posner. "Social Capital: Explaining Its Origins and Effects on Government Performance." *British Journal of Political Science* 28, no. 4 (1998): 686–93.

Bradbury, Bill. "Vote-by-Mail: The Real Winner Is Democracy." *Washington Post,* January 1, 2005, Editorial, A23.

Braithwaite, Valerie, and Margaret Levi. *Trust and Governance.* New York: Russell Sage Foundation, 1998.

Brant, Martha. "The Sage of Indianapolis." *Newsweek Magazine,* January 3, 2000.

Brehm, J., and W. Rahn. "Individual-Level Evidence for the Causes and Consequences of Social Capital." *American Journal of Political Science* 41 (1997): 999–1023.

Brooks, Arthur C. "Can Nonprofit Management Help Answer Public Management's Big Questions?" *Public Administration Review* 62, no. 3 (2002): 259–66.

———. "Is There a Dark Side to Government Support for Non-profits?" *Public Administration Review* 60, no. 3 (2000): 211–18.

Clarke, Richard. *Against All Enemies: Inside America's War on Terror.* New York: Free Press, 2004.

Coleman, James. "Social Capital in the Creation of Human Capital." *American Journal of Sociology* 94, no. S1 (1988): 95.

Coleman, J. S. *Foundations of Social Theory.* Cambridge, MA: Harvard University Press, 1990.

Coontz, Stephanie. *The Way We Never Were: American Families and the Nostalgia Trap.* New York: Basic Books, 1992.

Cotsgrove, S. *Catastrophe or Cornucopia: The Environment, Politics and the Future.* Chichester: John Wiley, 1982.

Crenson, Matthew A., and Benjamin Ginsberg. *Downsizing Democracy: How America Sidelined Its Citizens and Privatized Its Public.* Baltimore: Johns Hopkins University Press, 2002.

Cummins, Bud. "How Bush's Justice Department Has 'Blown It.'" *Salon*, March 31, 2007. http://www.salon.com/opinion/feature/ 2007/03/31/cummins/ (accessed August 26, 2008).

Dannin, Ellen. "To Market, to Market: Caveat Emptor." In *To Market, to Market: Reinventing Indianapolis*, ed. Ingrid Ritchie and Sheila Suess Kennedy, 1–55. Lanham, MD: University Press of America: 2001.

Dean, John. "Missing Weapons of Mass Destruction: Is Lying about the Reasons for War an Impeachable Offense?" *Findlaw's Legal Commentary*, June 6, 2003.

Delhey, Jan, and Kenneth Newton. "Who Trusts?: The Origins of Social Trust in Seven Societies." *European Societies* 5, no. 2 (2003): 93–137.

Dixit, Jay. "The Ideological Animal." *Pyschology Today*, January 2007. http://www.psychologytoday.com/articles/pto-20061222 -000001.xml

Dowd, Maureen. "Voting for a Smile." *New York Times*, January 6, 2008.

Duquette, Christopher, and David Schultz. "One Person, One Vote and the Constitutionality of the Winner-Take-All Allocation of Electoral College Votes." *Tennessee Journal of Law and Policy* (Spring 2006).

Dworkin, Ronald. "Constitutionalism and Democracy 1." *European Journal of Philosophy* 3, no. 1 (1995): 2–11.

Epstein, R. A. *Simple Rules for a Complex World.* Cambridge, MA: Harvard University Press, 1995.

Friedman, Thomas. "Obama on the Nile," *New York Times,* June 11, 2008.

Fukuyama, Francis, and IMF Institute. "Social Capital and Civil Society." International Monetary Fund Institute, 2000.

Galston, William A. *Liberal Purposes: Goods, Virtues, and Diversity in the Liberal State.* Cambridge: Cambridge University Press, 1991.

Gitlin, Todd. *The Intellectuals and the Flag.* New York: Columbia University Press, 2006.

Gittell, Marilyn. *Limits to Citizen Participation.* Beverly Hills, CA: Sage Publications, 1980.

Goldsmith, Stephen. "Moving Municipal Services into the Marketplace." *Carnegie Council Privatization Project,* no. 14 (November 20, 1992).

———. *The 21st Century City.* Washington, DC: Regnery Publishing, 1997.

Gray, John. *Men Are from Mars, Women Are from Venus: A Practical Guide for Improving Communication and Getting What You Want in Your Relationships.* New York: HarperCollins, 1992.

Green, John. "U.S. Religious Landscape Survey." *Pew Forum on Religion and American Life,* February 2008.

Gregory, R. J. "Social Capital Theory and Administrative Reform: Maintaining Ethical Probity in Public Service." *Public Administration Review* 59, no. 1 (1999): 63–64.

Haase, D. L. "Goldsmith Says City Innovation Has Its Price." *Indianapolis Star,* December 4, 1996, C1.

Hais, Michael, and Morley Winograd. "Millennials Are about to Give American Politics an Extreme Makeover." February 7, 2006. http://www.huffingtonpost.com/michael-hais-and-morley-winograd/millennials-are-about-to-_b_85556.html (accessed August 30, 2008).

Hagedorn, J. M., and B. Rauch. "Variations in Urban Homicide." Paper presented at the City Futures Conference, Chicago, 2004.

Rawls, John. "The Law of Peoples." *Critical Inquiry* 20, no. 1 (1993): 36.

———. *Political Liberalism*. New York: Columbia University Press, 1993.

Reagan, Ron. "The Case against George W. Bush." *Esquire*, September 1, 2004.

Remondini, David. "Goldsmith Looking to Cut City Force by Twenty-five Percent." *Indianapolis Star*, November 26, 1991.

Rich, Joseph D. "Bush's Long History of Tilting Justice." *Los Angeles Times*, March 29, 2007.

Ritchie, Ingrid, and Sheila S. Kennedy. *To Market, to Market: Reinventing Indianapolis*. Lanham, MD: University Press of America, 2001.

Romine, Van. *Civic Participation, Social Capital and Leadership*. Upland, CA: La Jolla Institute, 1998.

Rosenbloom, D. H., and J. D. Carroll. *Constitutional Competence for Public Managers: Cases and Commentary*. Itasca, IL: FE Peacock Publishers, 2000.

Rosenblum, Nancy L., and R. C. Post. *Civil Society and Government*. Princeton, NJ: Princeton University Press, 2002.

Salamon, Lester M. "Partners in Public Service: The Scope and Theory of Government-Nonprofit Relations." *Nonprofit Sector: A Research Handbook* (1987): 99–117.

Saletan, William. *Bearing Right: How Conservatives Won the Abortion War*. Berkeley: University of California Press, 2004.

Sandel, Michael J. *Democracy's Discontent: America in Search of a Public Philosophy*. Cambridge, MA: Belknap Press, 1996.

Savage, Charlie. "Bush Challenges Hundreds of Laws: President Cites Powers of His Office." *Boston Globe*, April 30, 2006.

Savolainen, Jukka. "Inequality, Welfare State, and Homicide: Further Support for the Institutional Anomie Theory." *Criminology* 38, no. 4 (2000): 1021–42.

Schlesinger, Arthur, Jr. "The Cult of Ethnicity, Good and Bad." *Time* 26 (1991).

Shapiro, I. "What New CBO Data Indicate about Long-Term Income Distribution Trends." Center on Budget and Policy Priorities, March 7, 2005. http://www.cbpp.org/3-7-05tax.htm.

Shear, Michael D., and Tim Craig. "Allen on Damage Control after Remarks to Webb Aide." *Washington Post*, August 16, 2006, A1.

Smith, M., Lionel J. Beaulieu, and Ann Seraphine. "Social Capital, Place of Residence, and College Attendance." *Rural Sociology* 60 (1995): 363–80.

Smith, Stephen Rathgeb. "Government Financing of Nonprofit Activity." *Nonprofits and Government: Collaboration and Conflict* (1999): 177–210.

Smith, Stephen Rathgeb, and Michael Lipsky. *Nonprofits for Hire: The Welfare State in the Age of Contracting*. Cambridge, MA: Harvard University Press, 1993.

Spicer, M. W. *The Founders, the Constitution, and Public Administration: A Conflict in Worldviews*. Washington, DC: Georgetown University Press, 1995.

Stern, William M. "We Got Real Efficient Real Quick." *Forbes*, June 20, 1994.

State Board of Accounts. "Special Report of Construction Projects for Franklin-Edgewood Park, Krannert-King-Brookside Aquatic Centers, and Perry Park Ice Rink and Aquatic Facility." September 16, 1999.

———. "Special Report of Construction Projects for Municipal Gardens Recreation Center and Carson Park Recreation Center." September 16, 1999.

Stier, Marc. "Principles and Prudence: Reconciling Liberalism and Communitarianism." Paper delivered at Annual Meeting of the American Political Science Association, August 31–September 3, 2000, Washington, DC.

Stolle, D., and T. R. Rochon. "Are All Associations Alike?" *Beyond Tocqueville: Civil Society and the Social Capital Debate in Comparative Perspective* (2001): 143–56.

Sullivan, Winifred. "The State." In *Themes in Religion and American Culture*, ed. Philip Goff and Paul Harvey, 257. Chapel Hill: University of North Carolina Press, 2004.

Susskind, Ron. *The Price of Loyalty: George W. Bush, the White House, and the Education of Paul O'Neill*. New York: Simon & Schuster, 2004.

Thompson, Clive. "Can You Count on These Machines?" *New York Times*, January 6, 2008, 40.

Tierney, John. "Facts Prove No Match for Gossip." *New York Times*, October 16, 2007.

Tocqueville, Alexis de. *Democracy in America*, ed. J. P. Maier, trans. George Lawrence. Garden City, NY: Anchor Books, 1969.

Turner, Margery Austin, and Julie Fenderson. "Understanding Diverse Neighborhoods in an Era of Demographic Change." Fannie Mae Foundation & Urban Institute, June 2006.

Tyler, Tom. "Trust and Democratic Governance." *Trust and Governance* (1998): 269–94.

Ullmann, Harrison. "Revolution: A City Where the People Are the Problem." *NUVO Newsweekly*, May 27, 1998.

Verba, S., K. L. Schlozman, and H. E. Brady. *Voice and Equality: Civic Voluntarism in American Politics*. Cambridge, MA: Harvard University Press, 1995.

Williams, Brian. "Our Fiscal Future Will Be Challenge for Next Mayor." *Indianapolis Business Journal*, November 1–7, 1999.

Wills, Garry. "Putnam's America." *American Prospect* 11 (2000): 16.

Wuthnow, Robert. *Loose Connections: Joining Together in America's Fragmented Communities*. Cambridge, MA: Harvard University Press, 1998.

———. "Religious Involvement and Status-Bridging Social Capital." *Journal for the Scientific Study of Religion* 41, no. 4 (2002): 669–84.

Wuthnow, Robert, H. K. Anheier, and J. Boli. *Between States and Markets: The Voluntary Sector in Comparative Perspective*. Princeton, NJ: Princeton University Press, 1991.

Wuthnow, Robert, and J. H. Evans. *The Quiet Hand of God: Faith-Based Activism and the Public Role of Mainline Protestantism*. Berkeley: University of California Press, 2002.

Yankelovich, Daniel. *Coming to Public Judgment: Making Democracy Work in a Complex World*. Syracuse, NY: Syracuse University Press, 1991.

Zakaria, Fareed. *The Future of Freedom: Illiberal Democracy at Home and Abroad*. New York: W. W. Norton & Company, 2004.

Zerubavel, Eviatar. *Social Mindscapes: An Invitation to Cognitive Sociology*. Cambridge, MA: Harvard University Press, 1999.

INDEX